Blind Faith

My Life Changing Journey in China

Dr. Denise Y. Mose

Copyright © 2020 Dr. Denise Y. Mose

All rights reserved. No part of this book may be reproduced or transmitted in any form or by any means, electronically or mechanically, including photocopying, recording, or by an information storage and retrieval system without permission in writing from the author of this book.

ISBN: 978-0-578-63713-6

Published by:

Edited by:

Spirit of Excellence Writing & Editing Services, LLC

www.TakeUpThySword.com

Dedication

You! My book is dedicated to you. Do NOT waste your life. Consider an adventure and see where it leads. You know you've thought about it. What are you waiting for? If you don't do it, it won't get done. Narrow down your options, decide, set a deadline, cut your losses, book the trip and GO!

My Eternal Yellow Butterfly...

2005 was the worst year of my life. My beautiful mother left this earth. However, she instilled priceless skills in me to last a lifetime. Since her passing, I have achieved quite a lot. Is this bragging? No, it is simply honoring what she always knew about her children. My mother loved yellow and she also had a thing for butterflies. Whenever I see a yellow butterfly, I know she's near and paying close attention...

My Hero

It's almost a shame. Honestly, it's just not fair. I have had Daniel Mose, Jr. my entire life. He wears many titles: Deacon, Coach, Leader, Chef, Handyman and Husband. My favorite title for him is simply, Dad. Do you have anyone in your life that has NEVER missed those key moments? I do. That person is my father. This portion of my book is dedicated to you, Father Mose. No words will ever be enough to thank you for a life of love, protection, laughs, discipline and knowledge that I will have for the rest of my life.

Cool Clique

Danny and Danielle are my siblings. I tell ya, we are really tight folks. Danny is my older big brother and Danielle is my identical twin sister. We shared many memories at 433. I reference the address of our childhood home because only they really know the beautiful life we had with our parents. Danny would say it was a "fairytale" due to the unabashed love that was poured into us. Nell (her nickname), would say that we were blessed. I'm just forever thankful that the good Lord put those two humans in my life as siblings.

Foreword

You know...my sister is amazing. Hearing the phrase, "Fly by the seat of your pants" applies to her. I have never seen a person more ready to go, ready to learn, ready to push the boundaries or just plain old READY like Denise. She needs no prompts, not much information, and has complete confidence that whatever it is will work out just fine. After all, we are talking about someone who moved to China for an entire year without knowing a single sole there. We are talking about someone who started her own beauty skin care line aptly called, Simply D. Did you all know that? Then, she turned around and created Daniel, her own men's cologne line that sat on the shelves of some rather cool high-end plazas. Denise traded in teaching to become a Celebrity Correspondent, which put her on the red carpet at the Academy Awards in Hollywood! If that's not enough, she has a stylist named Latoya who sends her designer gowns on a weekly basis. Who does this? Me, I don't do this. I need an itinerary. I need to know what's happening from Point A to Point B. Not my twin - she never has and that's what makes her so gosh-darn cool. As her identical twin (I am older by 6 minutes), I was honored that she asked me to write a few words. Enjoy her book about Blind Faith.

Love you, Nese,

Nell

Prelude

Here's the thing: if you had told me that I would be living in China for over a year, I would have thought you were crazy. But guess what? That's exactly what I did. Look, life is short, right? Opportunities like this do not come every day. So either you've got to really be off your rocker to even consider something like that or you've got nerves of steel. And this chick decided to take a gamble on that girl in the mirror! I had to really think this through. Would this adventure make me better? After all, there is no way I would know unless I actually went. Guidance was clearly needed here so I did what I always do: I called my identical twin sister Danielle. Apologies right now because you will hear that name a lot throughout our written dialogue here in the very book that you are holding. She said exactly what I knew she would say, "GIRL! GET YOUR BUTT TO CHINA!"

Then I called my beloved big brother Danny. Here comes the second apology – mentioning my brother. For that matter, let me continue the excessive apologies of all the loves of my life that will burn your eyes while chatting about my life in China. Deal? Thanks.

So, why write a book, Denise? Well, I've got something to say. Also, it was incredibly epic, and I am here to go over every detail with my lovely fans. Ok, maybe that last part was a bit of a stretch, but I had to try. Geez, it's not every day that you pack up your stuff and move to Asia! Besides, many people were asking what the experience was like living abroad and I think this is the best way to express those memories. In a nutshell, it's one of the smartest things I ever did for myself. Now, I won't go into all the particulars here - that's what those chapters are for, folks.

At this juncture, let me just say: Thank you. Thank you for picking up my book and joining me on how I spent my life from December 2014 through January 2016.

Hello, I'm Denise. It's nice to meet you. I'm 5'4, brown eyes, chocolate skin with a serious cool short haircut.

Let's discuss my book: Blind Faith.

Table of Contents

Are You Serious?

Sell Condo, Rent U-Haul

Chocolate in China

First Impressions

I Love My Job

Foreign Friends

It's Been Three Months...Hello, Hong Kong

My First Chinese Wedding

Beijing

Six Months Already

Bangkok

Moment to Pause...Mid-Autumn Festival

Shanghai

Thanksgiving

Christmas in Dubai

It's Almost Over...Packing Up

Korea

Touchdown

Afterword

Are You Serious?

Nouchelle Hastings...Yep! She's the culprit. It must have been around August when we first spoke. It was all a joke – or so I thought. "You'd be great in China, Doc!" That's what she told me. See, Nouchelle was a world traveler and often went to the Far East on business. Little did I know she had a trick up her sleeve just for me. Now, I've been to tons of places - even abroad (London, Paris) - but not China! It is literally on the other side of the world! Nouchelle and I were at my dining room table chatting one day. She came over because she was in the neighborhood and I had just made some coffee. I forget how we got on the topic of China, but we stayed there for a while.

Here's a little backstory: By this point in my life, I was a bit at my whit's end. For those who don't know, I volunteered in my community and had given leadership to many of the boards. Also, I served as a Fashion Columnist for several notable publications. Furthermore, I was active in my church as a Diaconate ("Deacon" to you) and was in many ministries there. Lastly, *Urban America Today* was my weekly live Talk Show and it allowed me to travel to some pretty kickass red carpets. Not to toot my own horn, but here I go...Roy Eavins, II gave me such a wonderful opportunity to have my own show. I had never thought about doing anything like that. After five years, we were still having fun and I loved my crew.

But even with all of that great stuff, I was bored. I just felt like I had gone as far as I could go in Orlando. Oddly enough, I was looking for a real change. And I mean REAL change, but not China. What's so crazy is that I was always interested in living abroad, but more of a western place, somewhere I'd already been. After all, Danielle did this same thing right after we both graduated from college. She walked across the stage in May and boarded a plane to Paris in August! No one in our family had been to Paris, but here she was...MOVING THERE! That following Christmas, I went to visit Danielle and Mom traveled to Europe later that spring. I get it now. She was ready for a life-altering change. To this day, she speaks fluent French and is teaching her daughter Madison. I've always followed my twin. Why should this time be any different? I decided to go with my gut, and I trust her completely...

Back to Nouchelle...She mentioned that her call that night would be to a few administrators in Asia. She further asked me to consider being on the call and a Foreign Professor position. Geez, she was serious. One thing about Nouchelle, she didn't joke often so I knew she meant business. But you know what? I found myself seriously psyched about the idea of actually doing it....Living in China! I did not know anyone who had done that. Yeah, spending the summer in Europe was a trek that people did, but they always came back home. So, to really pick up my stuff and move that far both terrified and tickled me. I told her to count me in on the call...just to check things out.

6:45 p.m. arrived and my Skype Messenger pops up. A sharp guy with a close-shaven haircut, dark suit, nice glasses and warm smile greeted me. I was secretly hoping he would cancel - no such luck. In fact, he was fifteen minutes early; I couldn't escape. After we exchanged pleasantries, he jumped right into my flight plans to come to his school. Whoa! Whoa! Whoa! This was moving way too fast for me. Nouchelle asked me to prepare a few questions, and you better believe I did just that. Guess what? He had none for me. With the beauty of Google, who needs a resume? You can see all you need by a few clicks and all your questions are answered. Nouchelle, of course, had emailed him everything about me, including my three published books. So, he only needed one thing from me: A signed contract to his school in Liushi, China.

After roughly 40 minutes, I didn't have any further questions for my potential boss. In fact, I was all the more eager to step into complete uncertainty. That night, I went to bed with thoughts of China on my brain. I'm surprised that slumber found me. The next morning, I made my usual cup of coffee and fired up my laptop. I'll give you one guess what I was about to do...Yep! I looked up Liushi, China. This is the first thing that I saw: **7,738 Miles**. Ummm, miles? 7,738 miles from home. 7,738 miles from my family. 7, 738 miles from the United States! 7,738 miles from my teenagers I mentored. 7,738 miles from my church. 7,738 miles from the sunny Florida beaches. 7,738 miles from...all of it.

Then I saw the population of China - It was just shy of two billion people. The good thing was that I had time to allow this to marinate. I did not have the job yet and he had a few other people to consider, so no need to pack my bags. However, I do not believe in coincidence - I was meant to talk to him and that was going to lead somewhere. My gut told me exactly where, I just wasn't sure I had fully embraced what was clearly my destiny...

Three days passed. Nouchelle calls me and says it's basically a done deal. Before we go any further, you need to understand something: Three is my absolute favorite number. Heart-pounding things have happened to me and they all have to do with this number: 3. I'm just saying - its magical and has special powers in my life. I chat with her about the Skype call and she is over the moon. She goes into detail about my work visa and getting approval from the Chinese Embassy to live in China for a year. I knew you needed a visa to travel to certain places, but the Embassy? Approval? I was scared! What did that mean? Was I going to court? I had so many questions. My comfort was that she calmed my nerves and told me I was slightly overreacting. However, if you were contemplating leaving everything you knew for a year to travel 7,738 miles away, you'd have a laundry list, too. Looking back, I know I would have never done this on my own; Nouchelle gave me the push to do it. I'm forever grateful to her because she knew I would be great. Sometimes, it takes someone else to see the potential we didn't know was even there.

Mr. Frank Sun and I chat, and he offers me a position at his university as a "Visiting Professor" in Liushi, China, for one calendar year. I'm utterly professional via Skype and we work out the details over a myriad of emails in the weeks ahead. However, on the inside, I'm doing a few cartwheels. I called my family, planned, and screamed around my condo: "Denise Yvette Mose is headed to Asia!"

I'm ready for takeoff!

Sell Condo, Rent U-Haul

I received my letter. It's real. It's happening. It's scary....

Now I gotta make some serious decisions. A year ago, I bought my awesome condo in Maitland; a year later, I must sell it. I call my realtor and tell him the very cool news. We set a date and go from there. Keep in mind, the year is almost over and by this point, it's August. I am due in China by the end of December. Denise Mose has no time to waste. I had to move and then mentally prepare to fly about 17 hours to my new home...Asia! Not to mention, my dad was getting married in December, too.

Atlanta.

My cousin Cherie told me that I could stay with her until I got my paperwork straight in Atlanta. Nouchelle informed me that I had to go to Duluth, Georgia, because that was the nearest Chinese Consulate that could approve everything I needed. Plus, they would fast-track my work visa. Geez, I am so glad I had her to guide me through all of this. It's always the small details that can derail a plan, so I'm grateful that Nouchelle left no stone unturned. This is my life after all.

Duluth.

Enter my buddy Chris. I have known this guy from so many red carpets. The one thing I forgot was that he recently moved to Atlanta. This only helped in my quest to Asia. While Cherie let me crash with her, Chris offered to drive me to Duluth. He asked me every question in the world and made our drive so much fun. I tell ya, you really know who your friends are when you take a huge gamble on yourself.

We get to the city and I walk into the office. Emily greeted me and I saw a folder with my name on it taking priority on her desk. Cool, she was ready for me. The one thing I read about getting a work visa was that you had to surrender your passport. Uggghh! I did not want to do that because if it got lost, it would be forever to get a new one.

This made me nervous. However, she assured me that this was standard procedure and I had nothing to fret. What choice did I have? I was already in Duluth and it was now or never. I slowly handed her my passport, paid the expedited fee and waited three days (there it is again) to hear from Emily. She reminded me that my fee was non-refundable and that all "should" be ok. Furthermore, Emily stated that in three days, I needed to have a one-way ticket secured to prove I was going to China. Why go through the trouble if I wasn't departing? When we returned to my cousin's house, I called Nouchelle. Not only was she excited, her company sent me three options of flights to choose from. I selected my date and the next email was a confirmation of a paid for ticket to Wenzhou, China. OH MY GOD!!!!!

Three days later.

Emily calls me and tells me to pick up my work visa and passport. I stared at the phone minutes after we hung up and spoke. Was this real? Like, for real? Like clockwork, I called my dad. "Baby, I'm so proud of you!" I replied with a simple thank you. I don't know about you, but just hearing my dad's voice makes everything better. He always knows what I'm thinking and offers so much confirmation that it tends to scare me a bit. Dad passes the phone to my twin and we laugh for the next half hour. Danny sends me a text and asks if everything is good to go. I respond with several smiling face emojis.

Chris picks me up and we are headed back to Duluth, Georgia. I'm appreciative because I recall this day being so sunny. Quite appropriate, right? That's what I thought. We arrive at the Chinese Consulate and Emily has a huge smile on her face. "Are you ready to go to China?" is all she says. She passes me my paperwork to sign, takes a quick photo of me and shows me my approved work visa for Asia. Well, I'll be. It is freaking official. She told me that she was excited for my adventure in her homeland. Emily was her "American" name - her real name was Ming. She explained that "Emily" was much better for business than her given name. She had a point. Some rules just don't change. First impressions are important in everything. As I walked out and shook her hand, she told me she was proud of me. That made me smile.

I closed out all my loose ends in Orlando and booked my U-Haul. I put a post on Facebook that I was leaving and that I was giving much of my furniture away. That helped! Tons of people came by to help me pack up and friends took the furniture to families in need. I mopped my floors and vacuumed the carpet. At church that Sunday, Pastor Leroy Rose said a prayer over me and wished me safe travels on my journey to living abroad. I drove my U-Haul to church that Sunday because I was leaving that day. I decided to spend my last days in the USA in Huntsville, Alabama. One, my dad was getting married to Joyce Watley and I was a bridesmaid. Two, I had to get all my soul food delicacies in because I knew the cuisine would be quite different in China. Third, I needed to hang with my siblings and just laugh until I cried.

<u>I left for China that following weekend.</u>

Exactly what does one pack when they go away for a year? I didn't know anything about my new hometown. I was arriving in December, so it would definitely be cold - that much I knew. Did they have all four seasons? Would there be any "American" restaurants? Did I need to bow? At this point, I'm going off what I saw in the movies and that wasn't always 100% accurate. Nouchelle said that I would have at least one roommate. Would she be a foreign teacher, also? My apartment would be within walking distance and that excited me. All of these visions popped in my head and made me eager for this trip. Like always, I opened my laptop to get some ideas of what was absolutely necessary for China. Thirty days...All the sites I researched had a very helpful checklist of what I would need. I decided to bring clothes that I could mix and match each day. Also, I learned that my co-workers would be in uniform. Since I was the Visiting Professor, that was not a requirement. This didn't surprise me; I had read that many schools in Asia had students dress this way.

Several slacks, jeans, many sweaters, socks, toothpaste, toothbrush, bathing towels, my favorite soap, tons of lip gloss, hair products and many other necessary things were put in one big suitcase. I did not want to bring tons of luggage because I did not know the size of my apartment or my bedroom. A serious carry-on bag packed with snacks, fruit and water was my best friend. Also, I had three outfits in there in case my luggage didn't arrive or was lost completely.

It was now or never. The day arrived. I left the USA for the continent of Asia. Was I ready? Hell yeah, I was!

Chocolate in China

I handed my boarding pass to the ticket agent and shock was on her face. After all, it's not every day that you see someone with a one-way ticket to China. I told her that I was moving abroad and staying for a year. She applauded me and told me to take a lot of pictures. Little did she know, I take pictures of everything.

Once I arrived in New York, things started to make sense. Because I was traveling internationally, I had to walk to the other side of the airport to get to my gate. Luckily, I had a three-hour layover. That was helpful because that side of the airport was a few miles long. Then, I saw My Departure Gate: The flight attendants were not American. No one spoke English. My plane was called Air Asia. Mama, I wasn't in Kansas anymore.

Thanks to Nouchelle, my seat was a business class ticket. I had more leg space and got cooler treatment than the folks behind me. Hey, if I am going to spend 17 hours in the air, at least let me be a bit comfortable. The flight attendant made her announcement and that was that. I was flying to China.

We missed our connection of course. The captain said that because we arrived so late, we would be landing in Shanghai, we were supposed to land in Wenzhou. WOW! That was unexpected. My twin had been emailing me to ensure my safety in China, but I wasn't quite there yet. Due to the international rates with my phone, I avoided calling anyone. I emailed my twin about the situation and she immediately responded.

<u>My first night in China.</u>

I was in a hotel in Shanghai. My passport was at the front desk to secure that I would be on the first morning flight. Already, I wanted to cry. The staff didn't speak English and I sure as heck wasn't fluent in Mandarin. Yet, I trusted them completely along with the other 65 people who were stuck just like me. Scared, excited, hungry and alone…This was all a part of the process of my epic year abroad. Sitting on the bed, I noticed that the shower shoes had a cool dragon design on them. Snuggling my feet into them, I wandered over to the bathroom to find the other knick-knacks that were in my first Asian hotel room. A comb set, bags of tea and fresh towels were staring back at me. I knew right then and there that those goodies would be packed away in my carry-on untouched. I took my shower and jumped in the bed, scared to sleep. They promised at the front desk that they would wake us up for our flight and breakfast. It was dark outside and nothing looked familiar. No, I didn't sleep a wink.

Nine hours later.

A knock on my door by housekeeping told me that I needed to get up and prepare for the last leg of my journey. Once I dressed and washed my face, my phone began to buzz. Danielle Mose was calling me. I took the risk of a very expensive international charge and answered her. She was glad to hear from me and her voice served as comfort. Downstairs, I saw the people from my flight and we all followed the crowd to breakfast. Mmmm, it smelled really good. A buffet style room was prepared with several plates, chairs and waiters. As I saw the other people with their food, I was excited to see rice. The rest of the food had me at a loss. My solace was the coffee that perched near my table - She was like an old friend. Quickly, I poured some coffee and had the fried rice. Yum! Immediately, the driver came into the dining hall and told us our bus was there. My new flight buddies and I hopped on and we all went to our corresponding gates. The sun was bright and my flight was a short distance to Wenzhou.

I was truly Chocolate in China! But we hadn't landed yet...

First Impressions

I quickly found my seat on the plane and tried to relax. Somehow, I couldn't do that. Have you ever felt like you were being watched? As subtle as possible, I looked to my right. Eight pairs of eyes were looking at me. I'm sorry, looking is the wrong word - Full blown staring would be more accurate...Not in a subtle way, either. A simple smile and a nod of the head was all I did. Hunger was calling so I grabbed my bag and chose some granola, fruit and a drink. This amazed my captive audience, too. I was ready for this. Some foreigners would become somewhat of an anomaly. Most folks who travel to the Far East rarely go on sabbatical for a year. No, most foreigners (Westerners, in particular) visit Asia for business and networking. I get it though, someone unique sits next to you and you're at a loss for words. Someone like me - Someone Black. Throughout the duration of my flight, their fondness to look my way didn't change. I'm glad; it got me ready when we got off the plane.

The airport was beautiful. The architectural structure outside and inside left me a bit speechless. China was an epicenter of art deco design; everyone knows this. Yet, to see it up close really makes your mind bend. As I exited the plane, I smiled even more. Due to all that Coca-Cola I drank on the plane, the bathroom was my next stop. Hallelujah, the signs were in English. Did I say smile? Grinning was more like it! I washed my hands, combed my hair and picked up my bag. Then it happened again...

People in front of me kept glancing in my direction. The more they ogled, the more I realized something: They were not checking to see what was beyond me. No. These new strangers had their target...ME! A real foreigner truly caught them off guard. As I continued walking to baggage claim, my presence became, dare I say, louder. Descending from the escalator, I turned the corner and you would think Michael Jackson appeared. They followed me. Like, really followed me. I had one intention, I needed to find Tina, My Interpreter. Being the newest celebrity in town wasn't my goal; I was there for a job after all.

My new boss and I had connected before I boarded the flight and she knew about my missed connection. She was waiting for me at the airport and I told her I'd stick out pretty easily. She saw me before I saw her. After she described herself, I knew she would be a bit hard to locate. Thin, long hair, and a smile - Well, that was half of the female population in Asia.

Like clockwork, I found a seat and my phone rang. "I'm here and I think I see you!" said Tina. Slowly, I raised my eyes and there she stood. Hands waving, phone to her ear and hair flying. "You are Denise? The American? For our school?" Oh, joy! Whether it was the relief of talking to someone I (kind of) knew or just exhaustion, I hugged her. That caused a slight commotion. I would eventually find out that it is not the custom of Asians to show public affection. Obviously in shock, she smiled and escorted me towards the car.

My first impression of my boss was a good one. Repeatedly, she apologized for her bad English, but I understood her just fine. As I rode in the front seat, I took in the sites of Wenzhou. It was real. The drivers were all Chinese. The restaurants I saw had the distinct written symbols. I would later learn that this is called pinyin - They are referred to as characters, not symbols. Fascination had taken hold of me! You see this in the movies, but I was here in the flesh and felt the need to pinch myself to make sure it was real.

<u>I was lost in wonder.</u>

Liushi, China. This was my new city. It was a bright and sunny day, so I could really take in my new home. I saw them... I actually saw them! A RICKSHAW!!!!! The cart and the Asian man driving. Are you kidding me? They were everywhere. I looked at Tina and gave her the biggest shock I could muster. At first, she didn't understand, but she soon got it. We kept everything in her car, and I gravitated toward the rickshaw. Tina waved to one of them, he stopped, and she ushered me to get in. Tears ran from my eyes.

I was dreaming! Excited to have a foreigner in his cart, he took off! Geez! These go so fast; I had no idea. I laughed so hard. Talk about visons coming true. He circled around the block and brought us back to Tina's car. The grin on my face was massive. Tina spoke to him and I heard the word "American" and he gave me a smile, too. I'll never forget that moment.

<u>My new apartment.</u>

Tina stopped the car at a huge building. Little did I know, this would serve as my new home for the next year. We got out and she insisted on carrying my big bag even though it weighed more than she did. I allowed her to help me because I did not want to insult her. This was her first impression of me, too.

Three flights later, we landed at Apartment 401. Silently, I said a prayer and hoped for a clean place to live where I would create a lifetime of memories. I had no idea of what to expect but I was here, and it was now or never. Thank you, Lord!

A huge apartment greeted me. A fully-furnished living room, dining room, kitchen, two bathrooms (American-style), big windows and the best part: A washer and dryer! Yes! I hit the jackpot. My research had showed me that usually, foreign teachers did not always get such a swanky apartment. Mine was beautiful. I arrived first, so I chose the cozy room off to the right. It was around 3pm so it was still sunny outside. After looking at the other rooms, I just loved the whole vibe of this one. It was quaint and it looked like me: Plenty of closet space, big window, a clean white desk, and a television. The part that really got me was the bed. It was really, really low to the ground. Because I loved to read, I had heard of the term feng shui. It was synonymous with calmness, tranquility, balance and harmony. Here it was in person. Something else I noticed was that everything had a circular shape. The coffee table, dining room table and even the plants on the floor were in this shape. Also, there were tons of candles, which represented a person feeling welcome. My bed was diagonal from the door, a wood door, which was a sign of stability. Tina explained all of this to me while she showed me around my new home. To say I was in awe is an understatement.

Hallelujah! The bathroom was American-style! The shower was, too. Ahhh! Ok, I can stay here. This will work. My prayers were answered. Tina told me about the bathroom at work...I'll get to that in the next chapter.

After she left, I sat on my bed. Tears escaped from my eyes and I let them. I did it. I really accomplished this crazy notion of living in China. I was here. Realizing I could not remain here forever, I torpedoed to my iPhone and cranked up the sounds of Michael Jackson's "P.Y.T.!" It blasted all through my room. That made this dwelling feel all the more mine.

I felt queasy, dizzy and light-headed. The idea of hunger didn't cross my mind because of all the excitement. As if she could hear my thoughts, Tina was back at my door. My apartment had a camera that let me see all incoming visitors. Talk about safety! That was awesome! I buzzed her up and she asked if I was hungry. Also, she wanted to give me a tour of my school. I loved this lady.

Later on that day, Tina took me to the bank. I was wondering when I'd get the chance to do this. As we walked in, I felt it immediately: The looks. Everyone made direct eye contact with me and it pretty much remained that way until I left. I gave some of my American currency to Tina so that I could establish my official account. I knew to keep some money for myself because I had not received my first paycheck. I filled out the forms and signed where Tina instructed. Although I couldn't read a thing, I knew exactly what it was. How funny! I was in a totally different culture, yet it was very familiar. I was pinching myself so much, I ran out of space on my arm. Tina and I walked to the counter and stood in line. What happened next took me completely by surprise.

As the teller invited us to the window, we didn't go alone. I felt someone next to me. And not in a casual way; no, she was nearly my shadow. I looked at her and smiled. The teller began to ask questions and my visitor stood right there as if she were a part of this conversation. This became uncomfortable. I raised my hand as if to move her and she looked confused. Tina caught this and explained to her that I was American. The folks in the USA are accustomed to personal space. Guess what? Not in China. I didn't know this. In Asia, it's quite normal to be very close to your neighbor without any inhibition. I took a mental note of this. Tina said that she did not mean any harm and just wanted to get a better look at me. Wow! Culture shock...

I Love My Job

French fries and pizza...Are you kidding me? I laughed. She had pre-ordered for us before we arrived at the restaurant. I took a mental note that this was probably the norm: the boss orders for everyone and that's the deal. Tina told me that she had to leave and that Laura would serve as my "go-to" person. A young woman with a sleeked-back ponytail and big smile walked through the door. Either the Chinese are extremely time conscious or there was a crystal ball somewhere. She sat down next to Tina and the introductions began. Laura spoke perfect English and that was another comfort. Also, she used a few slang terms and I immediately knew that we would be close!

Laura and I left the restaurant and turned a couple of corners. I did not know where I was going, but I was able to recognize my apartment building up ahead. Just like that, she stopped. "Here we are," she said. Oh, my goodness. There they were. The pretty red lanterns that you always see associated with Asia. Not only were they huge, but there were three of them. So many symbolisms caught my attention and I made a mental note of all of them. Laura and I walked into the building and she pushed the number three. The third floor? Ha! My favorite number. Immediately, I smiled to myself and remembered that God has a sense of humor. The doors open, and I see the words "George English School." Up unto this point, I did not know the name of the school, because there were three that I got to choose from.

We walked further in and the vision took my breath away. Bright orange, white and elegant office furniture caught my eye. To my right were clear glass offices. To my left was an open area of round tables, a high-tech LCD projector, state-of-the-art white board and brand-new advertising on the walls. Tina mentioned that the school was only a week old. As you enter the school, there is a huge half circle and I see that it's the front desk. I'm truly impressed. Laura takes me around the corner to a very stylish spot that is set up with computers, chairs and a printer. Black and red are the colors that serve as the backdrop and all I can smell is the newness. She asks me to pick my desk and I pick the one that's closest to me. It's facing the big common area and I like that. While checking out my new desk I see a row of curtains behind glass. I wonder what is in this big room near me. I walk over to it and open the glass door. Are you kidding me? A Theater? For real? I've already pinched myself, so I am seeing what else I can do to make sure this is all real.

Laura sees my shock and tells me that the owners have spared no expense in the needs for their new students to understand English. The breakroom/kitchen is on the opposite side of my office. I cross the front desk and go around another corner. She casually told me that she read how Americans love to bring their lunch to work. I thought this was so cute. Laura told me that most of the staff orders their lunch every day and that if I wanted to do this I could. Of all the things that Laura introduced me to at work, it was the hot water machine that shocked me the most. She told me I would need a thermos to drink my hot water.

Hot water? Why would I do that? Laura explained that Asians drink warm/hot water for a few reasons. It removes toxins from the body. Next, it hydrates you all day. Third, it allows their culture to maintain their signature slim shape. I did not see myself doing this. However, her explanations made sense and I honestly don't know of any Asians who have weight issues unlike in my country.

It was time. I had to ask...Where were the bathrooms? This was the one thing that I had to wrap my head around. When you move away from familiarity to an unknown culture, you accept the changes it provides. If you cannot do that, then please don't make this life-change. The restrooms in the Far East were the one area that took me the longest to grasp. You see, they are flat to the ground. No commode and no toilet seat. I saw the pictures before my trip and found myself giddy at how this was going to pan out.

Laura saw the apprehension on my face and she smiled. Slowly, I walked into the bathroom. Now, if you didn't know any better, you'd think it was a regular American (Western-style) bathroom, but no. As I went to one of the stalls, I saw it. Very clean and most definitely and emphatically flat. This was it, huh? My bathroom for a year...at work at least.

A positive mindset is everything. Once you tell yourself that something will be ok, the universe works to ensure that will happen. New apartment, gorgeous school, exciting topics to cover, foreign students. It was like 24-carat gold! This is how I was treated my entire time in China: I was a Rockstar.

Yeah! I think I'm going to love it here.

Foreign Friends

Laura, Ivy, Fred, Juan, Damian, Lis, Augustin, Dan, Sue, Sammi and Peter. I have no words, none. These are the people I will stay in contact with until the end of time. Let me introduce you to each one of them:

Laura...

My first meal in China was with Laura. We ate pizza, French fries and Coca-Cola. Laura spoke fluent English and she was even hip to quite a bit of slang. It was beyond precious to hear her say these words with her accent. Laura had graduated from college and was the Lead Trainer at my school. She knew I was coming and was excited to work with a foreigner. One of the biggest surprises was what she already knew about me. Laura had ordered my books, read my articles, and saw my social media posts. She knew me better than I knew myself. This was great yet spooky. The more I heard the conversations around me, I realized that I needed to learn some Mandarin. Laura supported this idea.

Every Tuesday from 1pm to 2pm, she was my teacher. Thankfully, we started at the very beginning. Meaning, we began with numbers, colors, days of the week and quick phrases. Luckily, Laura was a stern teacher. I eventually put these phrases on my wall at home to learn the language. Also, Ivy was a big help. Coupled with the Internet, I found some awesome lessons and cool apps to keep my Mandarin strong. Would you believe that I can still speak Chinese? Well, enough to get around without any help; and believe you me, that is an accomplishment. Mandarin is one of the most difficult languages to learn due to its tones.

Throughout the year, Laura and I shared so many great experiences. I honestly see her as a sister. As I was preparing to move back to the USA, Laura's family invited me over for dinner. It was a beautiful night. Last year, she had a baby boy. Guess who she named to be the godmother? Little Aidan is one year old and I couldn't be happier. I cried the hardest when I had to say good-bye to her.

Ivy...

Petite, sweet, loving, gracious and the nicest human being I have ever met. Ivy stands at a whopping 5'2 and weighs no more than 90 pounds. She is a walking almanac and single-handedly taught me her challenging language. Moreover, she was the third roommate. Turns out that everyone is not built for a year abroad. At only three days in my apartment, I had a few roommates to come and go. My parents always told me that once you make up your mind on something, stick with it - See it all the way to the end. Now, I am not saying my philosophy is better than anyone else's, but it sure helped when making this huge decision. The folks I met were from Africa, Argentina, Canada, Pakistan, Russia, Ukraine and everywhere in between.

Back to Ivy. She and I did not have the same work schedule. At George English, the Asian staff had one day off per week. Whereas, being American, we were used to having two days off every week (Saturday and Sunday). Well, that wasn't the case here. Saturday and Sunday were like any other day here. I found that both frigid and admirable. Ivy helped me prepare for my first week of classes. Honestly, I asked her what the students wanted to learn and her smile amplified. What was so great is that I had complete autonomy. Every night at 7pm, the school designated the open area as "English Corner" for whoever wanted to come. My first class was going to be Saturday. Whew! I had three days to plan. I decided to go with "Everyday Greetings" and have the students work in teams the last few minutes of class. My PowerPoint was prepared, and Ivy showed me how to use the high-end equipment for my class.

Stares...Lots and lots of stares...

Agape, awestruck, stunned, and down-right flabbergasted is how I would describe their reaction to seeing me. I smiled quite a bit and gave my background to them. After the novelty wore off, they seemed to warm up to me. Asians are extremely friendly yet terribly shy. This was going to be culture-shock for all of us. I used humor and that really endeared them to me. As I got more comfortable, I invited one of them to join me in a dialogue with the words I used on the PowerPoint. Nervousness was an understatement, but it soon became a fun task to try. Before the class ended, a few of them asked me to give them American names. I reached out for Ivy to help me understand. She told me that this was a big honor for the foreign teacher to give Chinese people Western names. I was both humbled and honored. There were quite a few named: Daniel, Madison, Lizzy, John, Michael and a couple of Denise's!

<u>Fred...</u>

Another Black person? Not only in China, but in my school! Yes! I could not believe my eyes. How do I portray Fred? Let's see: afro, tall, funny, educated and academically-sound. He had been off for two days and when he saw me, we ran to each other. Turns out he was from Africa and spoke fluent Mandarin! He was my new best friend besides Ivy. Being that he was Chocolate like me, I didn't even have to hide the few fears I had left. He had lived in China over two years and knew the city of Liushi in every aspect. Also, we had the same work schedule, which was perfect. He took me to the best places to eat and eventually, taught me some cool phrases. Fred told me that he was glad I made the leap to travel to China. I kept hearing that word: Proud. People felt this way about what I had done. Honestly, I saw it as trip of a lifetime, but that word often reared its head. After a while, I got used to it. After five months, Fred was assigned to another school. I don't have to tell you how heartbroken I was to hear this. Yet, I wished him well and we are still in contact to this day.

<u>Juan...</u>

Argentina sent its best to China. We had decided on doing our beloved "English Corner" at a local coffee shop that evening. It was here when Tina told me a new foreign teacher would be arriving. She said his name was Juan. I didn't know him, but I knew we would become the best of friends. At this point, I had been in China for about three months. Winter was slowly going away, and spring was around the corner. As I was teaching, Tina walks in with this tall, short-haired guy who had a nice smile. I paused the class and

Tina introduced him. Later that evening, we spoke and hit it off immediately. Because we had a few teachers to come and go, I ended up being the new Trainer for the foreign teachers. The next day, Juan and I had lunch and I spoke in Chinese. The look on his face made me smile. Those nightly lessons with Ivy were paying off. I wanted to learn this language and where better than with someone who was new like me. Turns out, Juan was a writer, too. His work contract was very brief and around September, he flew back home. Thanks to the power of social media, we speak on a weekly basis.

Damien...

If there was a heartthrob in my school, it was Damien. Olive skin, short black hair, slim build, charming and fluent in Mandarin. That's a tough combination. Pakistan sent us this very cool foreign teacher and he was popular immediately. The funniest way that Damien broke the ice with us was to dispel any stereotypes. Let's face it, we all have preconceived notions of each other. I thought this was a valid idea and it worked. Because I was American, they automatically assumed I was a spoiled brat. This was hilarious. However, it was good to see how other countries saw my beloved homeland. I asked Juan if he got tired of people always saying, "Don't cry for me, Argentina!" Damien loved the same kind of music I did: Michael Jackson! He loved "Billie Jean" and I worshipped "P.Y.T.!" Yeah, we all got along quite swell.

As the days went on, there seemed to be more females attending Damien's classes than anyone else's. And we all knew why: Damien was very good-looking. Clad in a black leather jacket (almost every day), designer jeans and an easy rockstar persona made him very popular. Let's not forget that he could go back and forth between English and Chinese. We encouraged the class to mostly use English, because that would make them stronger in it. Damien flew home, and I warned him not to come back without blessing me with some authentic Pakistani bangles! A week later, he brought back these gorgeous green bangles and I screamed. Shortly after that, he finished his contract. Another awesome person that I met on this epic journey.

Lis...

Tall, funny, well-traveled and super nice. How do I tell you about Lis? Well, for starters, he made sure I saw all the nuances of China. Meaning, he took me to the places that aren't even on the map. Like many people, I met him when he took my class. He was hard to miss, standing at over 6'7 with short black hair. He was fascinated that I was American and was in his world. I shared with the group that I wanted to see everyday life in China. Soon after class, Lis offered to travel with me. He had written down all the things I said I wanted to see. He worked for himself, so his schedule was open to serve as my tour guide. My next off day, we hatched a plan.

First up, the city of Ningbo. Lis told me that Ningbo was home to many foreigners who were brown like me. Also, he mentioned that Ningbo had some of the most historic temples in China and we could observe the monks who lived there. On the inside, I was screaming. It was one thing to hear about these places; it was altogether different to know I'd be seeing them very soon. Moreover, Lis was the first person to take me on the bullet train. The famous BULLET TRAIN! It is considered one of the fastest and quietest trains in the world! China is known for its serious advancements in technology and agriculture. I'm a witness that this is true. There is no way I can tell you all that we did. When I see you on my next book tour, I'll be sure to go into more detail.

On one of our trips, Lis did not tell me where we were going until we arrived. But he assured me I'd be excited. I'll give you one guess where we went. Got it? Still thinking? Ok, I'll tell you. He picked me up around 9:30am and we drove up a big mountain. Getting dizzy was in my near future so I hoped we were close. After another half hour, we stopped on top of a spacious hillside. What got me the most was how green the grass looked. As I walked closer to the edge, my eyes began to water. Was I really seeing this? The rice fields of China. There they were...right in front of me. I was told that you had to appreciate these from above or a long distance. Truer words were never spoken. The angles, design, and the sheer poetry in the rice fields boggle me to this day. Then, I saw them in the fields - the farmers with the signature hats that they wear. Are you kidding me??? Was I dreaming? Stunned...I was stunned. Lis allowed me to take it all in and just absorb this amazing moment. Writing this book reminds me of the sheer magnitude of my year abroad in China. I'll keep these amazing humans in my life forever.

Agustin...

As they say, "the buck stops here." Agustin Mar was by far my best friend in China. When I say we did everything together, I mean EVERYTHING!!!! Around my third month, that's when he arrived. Tina told me that another American was on his way and that she wanted me to meet him. In fact, she took me to lunch in Yueqing and I was just fine with that. She orders for the both of us and in walks this guy who I swore was Chinese. Once you see him, you'll know what I mean. Turns out Agustin is from Mexico and was hired to teach in China. After a big smile and a hug, I knew we'd hit it off. As a foreign teacher, each person has their own contract. Agustin lived on campus with his students and ate in the cafeteria. I immediately wanted to see what this looked like. Furthermore, he lived in a metropolitan city, whereas Liushi was authentically Chinese. Agustin had a Wal-Mart and Starbucks! That was a game changer.

My days off would be spent in the "Big City" of Yueqing. Massages, day trips, picking strawberries, meeting his students, riding on his motorcycle, shopping, climbing waterfalls, hiking mountains, grocery shopping, waiting for the bus, washing our clothes, going to the movies, clubbing, finding new restaurants and anything else that best friends do -- we did! In fact, Agustin threw me the biggest going away party on my last night. He was the hardest to say good-bye to. So, we decided we wouldn't. Thanks to social media, we talk on a weekly basis. In fact, I'm going to hang out with him in London, which is now his new home.

Dan, Sue and Sammi...

I had heard of the "hot pot" way of eating here in China. Reading up on the culture of Asia really helped me while I was in the air for those 17 hours. Three of the first people I met were students in my English Corner. Dan, Sue and Sammi were and are amazing. I addressed them by their "Western" names and they really enjoyed that. To truly inculcate me in Liushi, they offered to take me out to experience a hot pot. To say I was eager would be an understatement. There are just some things that are too hard to explain, but I'll try: Imagine a round table with a huge pot in the middle of it. When I say huge, that's what I mean. In fact, a whole in the table might be more accurate. First, they put oil in the big pan to get the temperature for the desired effect. Then, they bring the vegetables, meat, broth and other special seasonings that will go into your meal. The beauty of this is that YOU are cooking your food. Because this is the norm, I was amazed how they knew when to add which ingredient. In the end, you have the most delicious aroma coming from this pot and everything is in it!

Dan grabbed my bowl and got the ladle. I used my spoon and entered Heaven. Words cannot be formed to explain how yummy this tasted. My tongue was performing summersaults because this foreign food was pure joy. As we left the restaurant, we did Karaoke! Wow! I had no idea that this was so huge in Asia. We walked into this beautiful building and there were several rooms to choose from. Each room was themed, and I was smiling to myself. There were so many Western influences: Paris, London, Mexico and Italy to name a few. Although I had money, it was quite normal for the host to pay for everything. The food arrived and the music began. By the time it was my turn, they had picked nearly every American artist. I selected a Michael Jackson song and they all sang along with me. Another amazing night in China to store in my memory bank...

Peter...

Of all the people I met in china, Peter was by far the best dressed. That's due to his heavy love of my culture. Although he is Asian, he was a huge Hip Hop and R&B aficionado. Also, Peter was the assistant to the foreign teachers, so we worked very closely together. Plus, we laughed every day. When I first met him, he was wearing Levi Jeans, Timberland boots, and a fancy shirt. I couldn't believe it. After he showed me his music, I knew that we would be linked as life-long friends. One of the best things that Peter did for me was get me connected to my family via the Internet. I had heard of a virtual private network (VPN) but didn't know how to ascertain one. Because Peter is a tech genius, he took me to a store to buy a Chinese phone. Then, he helped me with the chip on the inside. By that evening, I was able to virtually see my father. I cried. Peter arrived around my second month and he remained with me until I left.

If I did not have social media, it would be difficult to stay in contact with all my foreign friends. I'm so glad that these people blessed my life. I hope I returned the favor.

It's Been Three Months...Hello, Hong Kong!

Multicultural, metropolitan, fancy, Western flair, modern and all things diverse - This was what I heard about Hong Kong. And boy was I ready to experience it. I celebrated my three-month anniversary in China by going to the Chinese Consulate. Foreigners had to do this to see how their experience was going and to talk to their country liaison. Tina told me that I would be flying in three days. What's so interesting is that Tina never asked me to do anything – she told me. I quickly understood that this was how business was done in Asia. In America, pleasantries are commonplace. You ask someone first and then wait for their reply - Not in China. I found this both exhausting and helpful.

Nouchelle informed me of the Hong Kong trip as well and encouraged me to take in all the sites. She also said that once the consulate met with me, I would receive another stamp in my passport in relation to my work visa. Geez! I had no idea. Furthermore, she mentioned that many foreigner teachers were sent back to their country due to questionable behavior abroad. I knew this wasn't me. But still, I kept my "nose clean" and was friendly to everyone.

I got on the train to Hong Kong and thanked the Lord above for such a time as this. I was here. Three months flew by rather quickly and I was having the time of my life. The more I walked the streets, visited restaurants, bought groceries, ate and just observed everyday life, the more I had to laugh. America has it all wrong about a lot of things that are associated with Asia. First, there are no "fortune cookies" given after any meal. I had no idea. They are not given out at all! This is an American tradition and to this day, I couldn't tell you where it comes from. Second, there is more than one language spoken in China. There is a dialect called "local language" and it's extremely difficult. I chose to focus on Mandarin, case closed. Third, none of the food in China tastes like what I had back in the USA. That makes sense, because the real stuff is here. Therefore, I refuse to eat any Chinese food (back in the USA) unless it is prepared by someone from Asia and I can communicate in the given language. Fourth, many people in Hong Kong do not speak Chinese. This made me think. You see, Hong Kong operates as an independent country. They have their own money and government. They speak Cantonese and not Chinese. My goodness, it's important to travel.

When I first went to Hong Kong, I was unaware of this rule. I used my Chinese currency to pay for the hotel and they simply looked at me. Due to Hong Kong being so used to global travelers, several people spoke English. The front desk assistant told me that my money was unacceptable. Because I was a foreigner, they were used to this. Thankfully, a bank next door had the exchange rate and I made my transaction there. Wow! Times Square (a take on New York) is the area where my hotel was in Hong Kong and it was simply gorgeous. The Butterfly Hotel would serve as my home for the duration of this trip. After I checked in, it was time to explore the city. Since I had a whole week, I decided to see a few historic sites.

First up: Hong Kong Disneyland. Oh, yeah!

Look, Disney World is a tradition in the USA. So, of course, I want to see it in Asia. The beauty of my hotel is that they provided tours to every cool site. This served me well the more I traveled throughout the Far East. I bought my ticket to Disney and my shuttle picked me up the next day.

Rain. What? Really? This was not going to stop my epic day of meeting Mickey and Minnie. On my drive to Disney, I kept looking at the rain. Silently, I prayed that it would stop because this was my only day to visit the theme park. Once I walked through the gate and showed my ticket, I saw them. I immediately felt like I was back home. Mickey and Minnie were greeting all the guest in the center of Main Street. As the rain poured, I purchased a poncho and got in line. Soon, it was my turn and the characters rushed to hug me. After several pictures were taken, I let them go and proceeded to enjoy the rest of my day.

But I noticed something: Even here in Hong Kong, people began to stare... "May I take your picture?" "Where are you from?" "Would you join us for lunch?" To be honest, I felt like a celebrity. When I say that people followed me, that's exactly what I mean. I would often look behind me and people were snapping my picture. Again, the novelty of someone so foreign was exciting to them. As they approached me, I acquiesced. Then, I smiled and made a mad dash in the opposite direction. The biggest surprise to me when people stared was something so simple: My skin - My beautiful ebony complexion. I was a chocolate chick in China, and they found me fascinating. Life is so funny at times.

Smaller and compact: That was my biggest takeaway from this theme park versus the one in Orlando. I mean, they had the huge castle, characters, rides and everything. I had to stop comparing it to the one in Orlando. It's not supposed to be the same, right? The Disney music blasted throughout the park and people carried Mickey Mouse balloons everywhere. I skipped to my next adventure and I got on a few roller coasters. The sun was peaking from behind the clouds, so the poncho had to go. All in all, I enjoyed my day trip to the park. I took several more pictures and headed toward the shuttle that would escort me back to the Butterfly Hotel.

The next day came and I met with the Chinese Consulate. Early was nothing new to me. As a professional educator for over 20 years, punctuality became my middle name. The driver picked me up in the lobby and off we went. The edifice was attractive to say the least. Stunning, big and intimidating. Honestly, I think the latter is what they were going for. This was an important building and high-and-mighty people were on the inside. It had to be a place where you took things very seriously. I walked through security and once again, I had to surrender my passport. I kept hearing, "American," and then they would smile while looking at me. Smiles are universal, that's why I use them. Once I passed the scanner, I walked to the elevator. As I stepped out, I came to a familiar place. I looked the photos up online and read how the process would happen. Since I had an appointment, my job was to watch the screen and look for my name.

Diversity was everywhere. As I sat there, my ears overheard so many accents. Where were these people from? A few I recognized, but some were truly foreign to me. A lady struck up a conversation with me and asked if I was American. Casually, I looked at the paperwork in her hand and realized she was a medical doctor from India. Cool! I nodded and inquired about her background. She was a pediatrician and was moving to China for three years. Beside her sat a little girl and she had paperwork, too. My mind was expanding by the day. Shortly after that, my name appeared on the monitor and a lady came out to find me. I stood, and she smiled.

After asking me several questions, she jotted down my response into her computer and took my picture. Then, she asked me for my passport. Because this happened so often, I always made several copies of my passport and kept them on me. I had heard horror stories of folks traveling abroad and no way to truly identify themselves. I took precautions to not be one of those people. She produced some more paperwork and asked me to sign a few documents. Of course, it was in English. Her expression was full of patience as she watched me read in detail everything that had to do with my name. My signature was required at the bottom. I asked her to give me copies of everything because I knew Tina would need the forms. Furthermore, these papers would assist in my certification after my contract ended. Lastly, she showed me my passport and two new visas. There it was! My ten-year visa to visit China and my expiration date while working in China. Dr. D was official! She released me, and I produced the biggest mega-watt smile that day. My shuttle was outside, but I decided to walk instead.

While I was outside, Hong Kong really showed herself to me. She was beautiful: Busy streets, music in the air, people chatting on their phones, a huge movie theatre, Starbucks to my left and very nice cars with few dents. Yep, you need money to live in Hong Kong. I decided to grab some coffee and people-watch. The hustle and bustle of people on the go does not change regardless of where you live. The owner of this barista was from Houston, Texas, yet resided here. Hong Kong was less stringent than China when it came to entertainment. There were some movies not allowed in China, yet very welcome in Hong Kong.

Interesting...

Later that day, I took the train to Causeway Bay. This is the heart of retail in Hong Kong. I was told it would be crowded and they did not lie. Every major designer label was here and the popular knock-offs, too. There were numerous dining options as well as bistro shops. From McDonalds to Levi's, it was all in this location. To my surprise, I lucked upon the Hong Kong Central Library. Since I always carry one of my books, I conveniently left it on the shelf for someone to find and hopefully enjoy. My iPhone had plenty of space to take pictures and I certainly made sure to capture each moment. Several purchases were made, and yummy ice cream was consumed by yours truly. I was having a ball! It was getting late and I did not want to get lost at night. I used my proverbial "Hansel and Gretel" memory crumbs and walked back to the train. The journey back to my hotel was quick and I decided to pack that night.

The following day, I took in all the sites of my hotel. I was in Times Square and there were some novelties in my immediate grasp. On the fifth floor, my hotel had a delicious restaurant. After sleeping in until around 10am my stomach told me it was time to get up. I dressed for the day and jumped in the elevator. Following my nose and hearing the clatter of plates, the elevator stopped and the doors opened. Every table was round and formally set for the next guest. Although I was by myself, they sat me at a full table. The waitress knew I had to be foreign and did her best English with me. Thankfully by now, I knew some of the best things to eat and was able to explain this to her. Pointing toward the buffet, she explained that this was part of the meal. Yeah! I saw the plates and starting piling on the grub. Coca-Cola was my drink of choice. After I satisfied my belly, I went to the third floor for a pedicure. A nice lady with a sweet smile pointed towards a chair. As I sat, she gave me the remote. Having so many options, I selected a few buttons which helped me further relax. Next, a young man brought out a tray of fruit to be eaten at my disposal. This was perfect. Forty minutes later, she was done. I went back to my room and took a nap.

Three hours later, I was hungry again. The small shop across from the hotel lured me in. The front desk manager said they had the best fried rice in town. Because it was around 3pm, I made the determination to bring food back to my room. This was going to be my last day and a lazy one at that. No longer able to resist the smell, I crossed the street to the boutique restaurant and entered. Fire, spices, smoke, and a long line were all good signs that I was on the cusp of deliciousness. My turn came and the older gentlemen spoke no English. However, they had pictures of food on display and I selected my photo. Fried rice, orange chicken and lo mein would do it for me. I couldn't wait to get to my room and tear into it. Because I had a fridge in my room, the portion size was more than enough in case I got hungry later.

I slept that night with a full belly. I rose the next morning and by the afternoon, I was back in Liushi. Throughout my year in China, I visited Hong Kong about five more times. What a fun city. I made a few friends and we flew to hang out. Just another epic footnote in my year abroad.

For my first time in Hong Kong, this was one of the best trips of my life.

My First Chinese Wedding

Tammy was a Trainer in my school. She joined us in the spring. I was adjusted to my schedule and more and more people came to visit what we had to offer. The buzz was growing that George English boasted having three foreign teachers. We were very popular, and it showed. The great thing was that each of us brought our own style to teaching the students. A young lady named Tammy was hired at George English and sat across from me. I was excited to meet her. She was refreshing because she didn't stare at me. Tammy lived in a bigger city so seeing foreigners was nothing new for her. Whew! Good!

I was knocking off a lot of things on my bucket list by living in China. However, I had always heard of the elegance that was associated with Chinese weddings. Little did I know, I'd soon be seeing this live and in color. Tammy's boyfriend had proposed to her and she invited me to her wedding.

<u>I had no idea...</u>

Culture is never-ending. The young ladies in the office were discussing the various traditions surrounding Asian weddings. They came to me to talk about what we do in America with regards to marital bliss. Ivy said that unlike in America, the groom can see the bride before the wedding. Also, a shoe is involved. The day of the wedding, the groom goes to the bride's house. While the groom is outside, the bride hides a shoe, typically red. I learned the color red is paramount in Asian cultures. Red symbolizes good luck, happiness and joy. Everywhere I went in China, I saw red dominate so many things. It is a color of extremes.

Back to the bride...She hides the shoe because the groom must find it. The family of the bride welcomes the new husband and he must locate her in the house. Once the shoe is found they are ready to start the wedding. This happens first and then the bride and groom go to their wedding together. I found this to be so unique.

The day came for Tammy's wedding and it was going to happen right before work. I had heard all about the glamour that went into an Asian wedding and it did not disappoint. First, it was held in a very expensive hotel. Second, her engagement pictures were stunning. Third, her invitations were on the prettiest stationery I had ever seen. I couldn't wait for this ceremony.

Tina said that she would pick me up for the wedding. Later, I found out that a foreigner can serve as good luck in certain settings. As we parked and got out, I saw several of my co-workers. Also, there were a myriad of people dressed for the wedding. As we entered the building, a few people asked for my picture. Juan and Damien were getting this treatment, too. Although my town of Liushi had a large population, it was not a Shanghai or a Beijing - Every nationality visits those places. Nope, I was still the local celebrity and in heavy demand. Tina loved this because she told everyone that the "American" taught at her school. I simply smiled and did my best to understand them. In the lobby there was a pretty basket of red envelopes. Oh, I could easily guess what this was for. Money! Looks like some of their traditions mirror the ones in America.

To say our table was perfect is an understatement. I smelled the fresh flowers before we even sat down. Then, I noticed our proximity to the actual ceremony. The bride and groom were going to be on an elevated stage, and we were right next to them. Wow! Tina told me that although it was their big day, being a foreigner had its perks. As the food was served a few people at the next table kept talking to Tina. I was busy chatting with my co-workers and taking pictures to really notice. After all, I had my VPN and was able to update my family and friends about my daily life in China. I knew they would be blown over by this showstopper of a wedding. Turns out, those people were asking if they could take a picture with me. This never ceased to amaze me. I was never offended by this gesture. Honestly, it made me realize that for some people this was a big deal. You can see someone of a certain culture on television but in real life, that curiosity is tested. Whatever stereotype they had, I was able to dispel it and greet each person in a warm manner. Once I took one picture, other guest asked for one, too. take more. Tina noticed this and asked our "fans" to kindly stop. This only happened when the food was being served, not during the wedding. Thank goodness.

The program proceeded, and I nudged myself a bit. Here I was taking in a very normal ritual, except I was in Asia. I decided then and there that if I needed to pinch myself for these cool adventures, then my arm would just have to suffer.

Tammy was beautiful and her groom was so handsome. Her dress left us all surprised. It was such a beautiful display of the color red. There were jewels, silk and so much detail in it. Her mother also wore a red dress and so did the groom's mother. The reception was held in the same room and people were ready to dance. Tammy and her husband went to each table and greeted each guest. We wished them well, hugged, took pictures and went back to the office.

I'll have those pictures for a lifetime.

Beijing

May...I was going in May. I counted down the days to my flight... Tiananmen Square, Temple of Heaven, Wangfujing Street, Summer Palace, Peking Theatre, The Palace Museum, Beijing Zoo, Jade Jewelry and a Wonder of the World: The Great Wall of China!!! I was one week away. The staff at George English told me to visit Beijing in May because these sites would not be as busy. Living in Orlando, I knew this all too well. Every Floridian knows not to go to Disney World in the summer - we make our way in the off-season...Less crowds and no blistering sun. It makes sense that Beijing would be the exact same way.

Carrie was a young woman who came to check out our school. She wanted to sit in our English Corner when the American (yours truly) was teaching. I was later told that she (like so many) had never met a foreigner like me. When my class was over, she made a point to stay after and talk to me. I told the class that I wanted to see all the historic sites in Beijing. Guess what? She was a travel agent. God knew what He was doing! Carrie offered to arrange my trip to Beijing. I was over the moon. Now, I was grateful, yet a little apprehensive. I talked to Laura and Ivy about this idea. They both said that she was very successful and would take excellent care of me. The next day, I emailed Carrie and this American was one step closer to Beijing.

Carrie didn't live far from me and that was a blessing. I took the short trip to her office and was super psyched to talk to her. She offered me coffee and it was delicious. We wasted no time. She had already shown me a few packages and all I had to do was pick the best one. To really enjoy my time, I decided on a full week in Beijing. I mean, Beijing is iconic, and I didn't want to be rushed in capturing every detail. When I left Carrie, I had my hotel, ticket and personal driver all planned. This last part was the best idea that Carrie gave me. When I explained what I wanted to see, she knew that I couldn't do a regular tour. When she mentioned a VIP Tour Guide, the first thing I thought of was cost. In actuality, she knew several people who were professional and would ensure that I got my money's worth. I trusted her and breathed a little easier.

The time came for my trip. Tina said that the students would miss my classes and asked me to make my stay only three days. No way! Yes, I was here to teach, but if I spent a whole year in China and did NOT go to the Great Wall, then I would consider that a wasted trip. Besides, in my contract, I had planned three major trips that would all be at least a week. I didn't know where I'd be going, but I knew one of them had to be Beijing! It was springtime and the weather showed sunny skies all week. I hailed a cab and told him to please take me to the airport in Wenzhou! By this time, I was traveling alone and my Chinese was good enough to get me around without assistance. I was so proud of myself. The cab driver spoke a little English so that helped, too.

We arrived at the airport and I found my gate. As I packed for my trip, I kept a few things in mind. Always carry your own towels. I had gone on a quick trip to a neighboring city with my co-workers and soon learned that the towels were in short supply. I did not make that mistake on this trip. Although my hotel had a 5-Star rating, this American packed her towels. This would serve as a critical tidbit of information on my trips throughout this year abroad.

As I boarded the plane and sat down, I smiled looking out of the window. I had made it five months in China. The time was starting to fly by. We landed in Beijing and boy was it different than my town of Liushi. While I rode in the shuttle to my hotel, the architecture got my attention. I saw cranes everywhere and they were building these epic skyscrapers. With my own two eyes, I was seeing this. The cab driver shared a few sites with me on the way, which was very nice. He showed me Olympic Village, which wasn't far from my hotel. I saw the Aquatics Center, or "bubble building," where Michael Phelps won his historic record eight gold medals in swimming. The building is truly a wonder; the outside has shapes in the form of bubbles, hence the nickname. Further on down, I looked in amazement. Beijing is a technological force and I was smack dab in the middle of it. The vacation was already off to a great start.

My hotel had a nice lobby and I smelled the food from outside. Carrie made sure to book my stay with a few restaurants attached and room service for my convenience. Hey, I'm American. We like it that way. The front desk was expecting me. As I pronounced my name and produced my passport, they alerted me of the restaurants and other great features. I took the elevator to my floor.

A beautiful suite awaited me on the other side of the door. Because I had Renminbi (RMB or Chinese currency), mama could splurge. So, I did! First, it was nice and cold. Perfect! Although it was spring, the weather was due to be hot my entire week in Beijing. Second, there was a big sitting area in front of my windows. Yes! Two leather seats, a couch and a very pretty desk. This is what I wanted. I knew I would be touring so my hotel had to be comfortable and relaxing. Thanks, Carrie! Next, my bathroom: Oh yes! Four people could fit comfortably in there! Tons of towels (although I packed my own), soap and other amenities were in abundance. Once I gave my room a thorough inspection, I headed downstairs to eat and confirm my tours.

The next day...

I was bright-eyed and bushy-tailed because this was the DAY I was going to see one of the most iconic sites in the world. Today was my tour of the Great Wall of China. Nothing was going to ruin this day. The weather was perfect, and I had my phone ready to take several pictures. Christine was my VIP Driver and she was right on time. This was going to be my practice from here on out. By having my own driver, I was not limited to a schedule. She was with me the entire week and we hit it off from the beginning. She told me that we would visit a few important places and end our day at "The Wall." Excitement poured out of me as we headed to see Beijing.

Jade's Palace was a jewelry store that many tourists visited. Christine told me that jade was an important stone in Chinese culture. As we walked in and saw the beautiful pieces of jewelry, I decided to buy a small jade bracelet. It fit my arm perfectly and I instantly fell in love with it. After that, she showed me a few other cool locations and gave me some information of places we would see the following day.

We traveled quite a bit and I noticed we were going higher and higher up the mountain. She gave a lot of history about why the wall was built and who it was meant to protect. Also, she explained the length of the wall and how long it took to complete. My mind was blown.

And there it was...

The stone brick, the way it bends and curves, the gray color, the sunshine beaming down and the majesty of it all...My mouth dropped open. Instantly, I thanked God for allowing me to see this with my own eyes. Was this real? THIS CAN ONLY BE SEEN IN CHINA, SO I HAD TO BE HERE RIGHT??? Christine noticed that I was speechless, and I faintly heard her say that the wall was nearly 13,000 miles long. As I watched the various ways that the wall was made, I couldn't wait to get out of the car and see it closer.

Christine drove through the entrance and parked the van. I saw several busses, shuttles and cars all with the same goal as I had. Something else that I found fascinating was the languages that people spoke. It was another reminder of how epic this "wonder" was to all people. With tip-toe anticipation, we trekked to the ticket booth and purchased access to walk the wall. In my hand, she passed me the final step to make all this come true.

Something I didn't expect was to see all the commercialism. I don't know, I just figured it wouldn't be like the typical Walt Disney World ride where you must walk through the gift shop before you are leaving your attraction. Here's the business side of my head: you don't see The Great Wall of China every day. Of course, people wanted a memory of it. There were so many shops, boutiques, and other knick-knack tables of items to be bought for each visitor who passed by. If you can't beat 'em, join 'em! So, I did. There was a photographer at the foot of the first part of the wall. He was capturing guests' first impression of the wall for a small fee. I paid him my price and got my pictures. Hey, you only live once.

As I turned the corner, Christine took me to the portion of the wall where all the tourists were guided. Because the wall is so massive, clearly you cannot climb all of it in a single day. Plus, wear and tear over time has allowed some parts of the wall to be limited or have no access at all. As I looked up toward the top of this side of the wall, I did not see an ending. Thankfully, it wasn't required to reach the top. Besides, I just needed to feel the bricks. Denise was in no competition here.

Now this was interesting: As I climbed up the steps, I noticed that they were not the same. When Christine was explaining how the Great Wall was designed for protection, she mentioned that the builders did everything they could to make it hard for their enemies to gain access to the highest levels. That makes sense because the steps range in size and depth. If you are not careful, you will trip and fall. I made sure to hold onto the railing as to avoid this possible outcome. You could see the markings in the wall and it truly humbles you. So many people were walking back and forth at the showcase of this jaw-dropping piece of history.

As I continued my goal in reaching the top, a tear escaped from my eye. I was here. I know I keep saying that, but I had to stop and breathe in this moment. I left my home, family, country, familiar surroundings, and jetted off around the world to live for a year in Asia. Who does that? This chick does, that's who. So here I was, standing at The Great Wall of China looking at what God had allowed me to see for this moment in time. Breathing in the fresh air with the sun blazing, I descended the wall. I purchased tons of memorabilia because who knows when my feet would touch this ground again.

Because I had achieved such a global milestone, I did the only thing that made sense at this point. I posted all my pictures on social media! In this day and age, instant gratification is necessary and convenient. Why not! Besides, the pictures of this Wonder of the World stopped me in my tracks. My twin tried to call me via my phone, but there is hardly any reception at The Great Wall of China! Because I was mesmerized by what my eyes were witnessing, my purchases increased tenfold. Christine did not rush me at all and that was the beauty of securing my personal driver. At that moment, I pulled out a photo of my family. I made sure to capture them with me at such a luminous occasion. Christine took my phone and I held up my family to my face. After all, without their support, I wouldn't be here. It's a small thing, but it means everything to me.

Three hours later, we hopped in the van. My mind was still reeling from my day. Did that really happen? Christine drove me to a spa in Beijing. I mean, once you climb The Great Wall of China, a massage is in order. The first thing I noticed as we walked into the spa was the beautiful pieces of porcelain. Oh, my! The owner of the shop greeted me and smiled. He spoke to Christine and I heard her say, "Měiguó," which means American in Mandarin. He slightly bowed to me and ushered us into a beautiful room. As soon as I sat down, a young lady brought a tray of tea and fruit. Christine was tired, too. She served as my photographer as well as my driver. She explained the importance of taking care of the body in the Asian culture. Also, she mentioned that serenity and calmness were staples in her heritage. I must say this was evident my entire time living in China. Some of the best tea I've ever tasted was from the Far East. After our massages, Christine took me back to the hotel to rest because that evening, we were going to Peking Opera! I said a silent prayer of thanks.

When I said that I wanted to see Beijing, I meant it. Christine picked me up at 6:30pm and we were off to the show. Who hasn't heard of Peking Opera? For those that don't know, it is a treasure to see. Peking Opera is the most dominant form of Chinese Opera and it incorporates the following: music, vocal performance, mime, dance and acrobatics. Since Christine pretty much knew me at this point, she grabbed my phone and started taking pictures. I wanted to soak up every piece of this night and reflect on it back in the hotel. The programs were passed out and we found our seats. I often told Christine that her presence was a big help to me. She provided a lot of backstory to everything we did and even took me to a few places that were not on my list.

The show began, and I could barely breathe. Such amazing characters and the costumes made you look twice. My seat was close to the front and that was good and bad. It was great because I got an excellent view of so many things happening on the stage. The only drawback was when one of the actors looked directly at me. They held my eye contact and drew me into the performance. The makeup used was deliberate and each person was unique yet beautiful. This was another "pinch me" moment. I had a whole week to enjoy this exotic culture and I was here for every experience.

After the show, we walked to and landed at Wangfujing Street. Unusual delicacies were one of the biggest things that this area is known to have. I just had to see what all the fuss was about. The more we walked, the better the food smelled. High-end stores were located here and each one looked spotless. Oh, and there were tons of people there to see the splendor, just like me. As we turned the corner, my eyes stopped blinking. I had seen pictures of the food, but it was quite another thing to see it in front of you. Deep-fried starfish? Snake on a stick? Seared caterpillar? BBQ spider? Fried scorpion and seahorse? What??? If I hadn't seen it with my own two eyes, I wouldn't have believed it. But there it was for all to see and to buy! Speaking of, the lines were long and the money flowed. To taste these items was not in my plans; the view was enough. In China, there was no waste. None! My friend Laura told me that, too.

I posted all my pictures on social media and laughed with Christine. We traveled to the end of the street and took in all that I was seeing. Eventually, we headed back to the van and sleep was calling me. Christine told me to get a good night's sleep because in the morning, I had to be ready at 6:45am! She was taking me to another place and told me I had to be quiet when we got there. I could only imagine what she was planning...

Coffee in hand, I jumped in the van with the best tour guide in Beijing. I asked her where we were going, and she simply said, "Trust me, you won't forget this!" We pulled into an empty parking lot and saw the signs for "Temple of Heaven." This replica is located at the Chinese Pavilion in EPCOT at Walt Disney world in Orlando, Florida. Yet, here I was seeing the real deal. As we exited the van, I heard music. Very soft and relaxing music. The one thing I noticed is that there was no noise, just heavenly sounds. I followed Christine inside this very pretty park, and I saw them...all of them...

Are you kidding me?

Several groups of Asians were doing all types of Tai Chi. There were women, children, teenagers, older men, and some people by themselves in the grass. I could barely contain myself. As I walked in and openly starred at all of them, I held onto Christine to protect my equilibrium. The further we journeyed into the park, I saw an older man and he was absolutely graceful. He had a long beard, no shoes and red silk pajamas. I was paralyzed - Literally, I couldn't move. This man was art. Christine told me not to stare, but I couldn't help it. Each group had their own steps for each song that played, and I was a kid in a candy store. Before I knew it, someone had touched my arm and invited me to join them. Immediately, I gave all of my belongings to Christine and did my best to mimic the steps they were doing. The lady moved my arms like hers and kept smiling at me. Giddy is not the word to describe what I was feeling. Denise Mose was in the moment and I released every happy feeling I had. Afterwards, instead of me wanting their picture, they asked for mine.

Jumping up and down from my morning experience, Christine took me all through the park. From the outside, it doesn't look that big; but once you traverse enough, you realize its magnitude. We followed the crowd to see the other special site that we were all here to see. What is so powerful is that there are steps you take that lead you up this juggernaut. The space is wide open so that you only focus on what is front of you. Distractions are eliminated.

There are many white steps, gates and railings to hold onto because you will need it. Literally, this vision takes your breath away. That's the cool part: the feeling of being someplace very pure and scared, because we were.

It didn't look real...

Yet, it was staring me in the face. The Temple of Heaven! Enormous is not the word and mammoth is a close second. The Temple of Heaven is an imperial complex for religious ceremonies. The emperors of the past came here to pray for a good harvest. It was also seen as a type of altar. My eyes kept going higher and higher because of its majesty.

The intricate details that made up the temple deserved my utmost attention. Several people bowed, said prayers, took pictures and simply touched it to make sure this wasn't a dream. As I floated closer, I saw that it was large at the bottom, too. As you made your way around the temple, you could see the unmatched physicality that made the temple so timeless.

Also, near the temple was a separate altar. It was circular, too. The sign read that it was called the Imperial Vault of Heaven. Christine told me we had to go in to experience my very own echo. Once inside you can whisper something from one end and your voice will transmit to the other end. I tried this and it was awesome. Like the other temples, people prayed here for healthy harvest, prosperity and wealth.

Because we got there so early, we really had the gift of seeing the sun as it shined its soft rays on this scene. I pinched myself again. As we walked back toward the entrance, I saw so many cypress trees. Christine told me that many of these trees were more than 600 years old. We touched them and took a few photos, too. By this point, the people who were exercising were now singing. Imagine several hundred people in a circle singing authentic Asian opera songs. I quietly joined in and stood with them as many other tourists did. This was our gift to hear them and observe the passionate lyrics. I had no idea what they were saying, and it didn't matter. We got in the van and I was ready for our next adventure. Christine told me to wear my walking shoes because this next one was going to wear me out. She didn't lie...

The Forbidden City! She parked, we got out and I just stood there. She told me that we had to go through Tiananmen Square first. Yes! I couldn't wait. Tiananmen Square was known for protests throughout the years and it sits in the heart of Beijing. It is the largest square in the world. Before you enter, you must walk through a metal detector and they have you discard anything that might be harmful. These structures are thousands of years old and the penalty to try and destroy them is taken very seriously. I carried a fanny-pack and that was all.

The square was immaculate. So many people were there, but you did not feel crowded. I think everyone had the same feeling: shock and wonder. You must first enter the square, go under the street through the tunnel, buy another ticket and then you climb the steps to be in front of the Forbidden City. I tell you, having a guide makes all the difference. Christine stayed with me every step of the way. Could I have figured this out? Yes, of course. She was a comfort and could pinpoint what to do and where to go - A real lifesaver.

Because the throng of people was so paramount, the guard kept a count of the tourists who entered. Our turn came and man, was it crazy! Everyone must walk through huge gate and pass the portrait of Mao Zedong. Christine bought the self-guided ear-piece ticket and that was incredible. When I saw the brochure, my hands grabbed ten more. My family was going to experience this with me when I got back to America.

The Forbidden City is a palace complex in the middle of Beijing. It served as the home of emperors and their households. Many ceremonies were held here and was the backdrop of the political center of Chinese government for almost 500 years. Here's the big question: Why is it called the Forbidden City? In the past, commoners were prohibited from entering the palace without permission. Only the imperial families and invited high officials were welcome. Furthermore, if the emperor was given bad news, the messenger could risk losing their life. In addition, if the food was not cooked the way that the emperor liked, the chef could face death. Moreover, I learned that only the emperor could wear yellow so if someone wore this color, it would be a bad day for them. During the Ming and Qing Dynasty, this was the case. Colors carried meaning and yellow was for royalty and high society. You see? Once you entered the palace, you didn't necessarily leave. Hence the name.

The walking tour explained all of this and my education of China grew by the minute. It was also here where I bought the famous Chinese Boading Balls. The Asian culture takes their health very seriously. These boading balls, or some say medication balls, are synonymous with your equilibrium. They are often used for putting pressure on the chi points in your hand, but they'll also provide you with a calming sense. Once you have two balls that fit your hand size, use your fingers to circle them around your palm. This is to promote serenity, tranquility and a Zen-like presence. I bought five pairs for my family.

There was no way we were going to get to all the domes in this city! I counted over nine separate palaces. Oh no! Plus, the ruins were fragile so the ground at some pointswas very unsteady. Three hours later, we were back in the van and my mind was exploding. What a day. I arrived at my hotel, ordered dinner and crashed in my suite. I had another big day tomorrow!

Who doesn't love animals?

We were off to the Beijing Zoo. I was eager to see all the creatures. However, I must tell the truth: The panda bear is extremely popular in China and today I was going to find out why. Before I even arrived in Asia, there were panda references everywhere. I asked Christine about this. She told me that panda bears were crucial to the bamboo forests by spreading seeds and helping vegetation grow. Education is everywhere!

Once we bought our tickets and took a picture by all the signs, we walked into the park. It was a gorgeous day and I had my agenda. The Beijing Zoo was huge, and I was ready. There were four animals that I had to see: The panda bear, giraffe, elephant and hippopotamus. My identical twin danielle loves the giraffe - She has since we were children, so that was a must. Next, the elephant. To me, they are so majestic and friendly. Who doesn't love an elephant? Lastly, the hippo! I must have been six or seven when I was gifted a stuffed hippo as a toy. I never forgot it. From then until now, it has served as my favorite animal.

We saw a myriad of birds, monkeys, fish, and other animals. The zebras were next and they were beautiful. Unfortunately, the lions were sleepy on this day, but I took their photo anyway. I mean, they are the king of the jungle. I saw signs for the giraffe and immediately increased my steps. The zookeeper said that we could feed them for a small fee. Of course, I paid it. Far be it for me to be in Beijing and not feed a giraffe. That doesn't happen every day! On cue, Christine started snapping the pictures as I approached a powerful giraffe. I want to say she smiled at me as she extended her long neck in my direction, or maybe it was the huge leaf in my hand that she was aiming for. In my mind, I am going to hope she was just glad to see me.

From there, we ran into the elephants - Powerful, strong, yet kind. I have always sat in wonder of this enormous mammal. Elephants are in the pachyderm family. Hooves, nails, and thick skin are just a few of their features. Let's not forget that their weight is just shy of around 13,000 pounds. And yet with all of that, they are some of the sweetest creatures. In my chapter on Thailand (coming up later), I'll talk about how an elephant picked me up after my jungle ride. I could hear him laughing at me. I watched many of the elephants and her babies eat that day. They were beginning their show and I stayed to watch it with Christine.

Splash, splash, splash! I saw them! My favorite animal in the whole world! Ahhh, my beloved hippo! The hippos weren't paying any attention to my small frenzy and that was just fine. They moved at their own pace and were a joy to watch.

While enjoying my day, music kept playing throughout the park. And guess who was on repeat? That's right, The King of Pop, Michael Jackson. Isn't that a bit mind-boggling? Here I am in Asia and Michael Jackson is on the speaker system at the zoo in Beijing! If that's not global appeal, I don't know what is, folks! Christine and I jammed to "Billie Jean, "Thriller," and "Beat It." Very cool indeed.

As we went up the hill, the sign ahead read: Panda! We were almost there. Besides the lions, the pandas had the largest enclosure. I counted about six of them and they were big. They brought out the baby pandas for the tourists and when I tell you they were adorable, they truly were. I made it a point then and there to buy a panda stuffed animal for my niece Madison that day. Like clockwork, we ran into a gift shop dedicated to the panda bear. Perfect!

My vacation in Beijing was everything I wanted. The iconic sites that I wanted to see and touch were ascertained. I spent my last day in Beijing shopping for mementos and simply enjoying the surroundings. The hotel had several restaurants and I feasted on the bona fide cuisine. If I could take some of this food back to America I would in a heartbeat. As I flew back to Liushi, more tears ran down my face. I was in a realm of gratefulness. What an epic vacation! A week in Beijing to see a cherished Wonder of the World and several other historical places. I couldn't wait to plan my next trip.

Six Months Already

Time flies when you are having fun and Denise Mose was doing just that! Geez, has it been six months? Yep, it sure had. Juan, Damien and I were loving our job. Our students were learning English more and more every day. We were proud.

One day, Tina walked in and told me something. Remember how I said she never asked me, she simply gave instructions. Turns out, I was going to be training Chinese executives twice a week. What? Not only that, but I would be doing this in the city next to mine, and they were going to escort me back and forth. My head was swimming.

Fifteen executives (male and female) wanted to learn English better. So, because I was the "Celebrity Foreigner" and an American citizen, I fit the bill. At first, I was against this idea. However, after further thought, I loved it. I could leverage this for myself back in the USA. Tina told me I could create my own program, activities, PowerPoints and anything else that would be required. That's the thing about Tina: if we needed it, she bought it!

The next night, a tall guy named Alex picked me up for my first class. The drive had to be a good 25 minutes. He played a lot of American artists and I hummed along in the backseat. As we approached the building, it was beautiful. Although it was at night, it was well lit and had expensive marble pieces out front. This was a pattern that I noticed throughout certain buildings in Asia. Banks, businesses, luxury hotels, restaurants and mansions showcased these mythical creatures before entering. On either side would be the shape of a large animal (usually a lion) with sharp claws. One lion, the male, would have a ball under its palm, symbolizing power and protection. The other lion, the female, would have a club under her claw that also represented protection from harmful spirits. I later learned that these were called imperial guardian lions. In the Asian culture, the after-life is critical. Because many Asians are Buddhists, this is the case. When I was in Beijing traveling, I saw so many mythical creatures and it was important for me to learn this part of their history. I tell ya, traveling is its own education.

Back to my class...

I am notorious for showing up early. My parents always encouraged us to be on time and that being the first one was a sign of preparedness. My copies were already made, and I fired up my laptop to their high-tech stuff. Moments later, several people came in and smiled at me, followed by a very nice, "Hi." Wow, they were nervous; I could tell. I quickly put them at ease by speaking some Mandarin and they got into my groove. Each person went around the room and told me their position in the company. Their English was quite good, but I could see why they wanted to brush up on some communication skills.

The hour went by rather quickly. I gave them a fun homework assignment to be due at the next class. They shook my hand as they exited, and my driver was waiting for me. I had to laugh: Here I was in China with a private driver and I had just trained executives in English. Isn't God amazing?

I was their facilitator for another four months. As the year progressed, they got better and better. They gave me a tour of their facility and my mind was in awe of the mass production done on things we use every day. The culture that I was immersed in was so wonderful. Living in China changed me; it made me better.

Ivy, my beloved roommate, mentioned that her family was going to "Tomb Sweeping Day" in the spring to visit her ancestors. I was peaked. She told me that this was tradition and that it usually falls in what we would call April. Furthermore, she made it clear that this was an important day to show respect to the previous generation. In the Chinese calendar, Tomb Sweeping Day, is the second of 24 solar terms of the traditional Chinese Solar calendar. Ivy mentioned that her family would make offerings that included the following: praying to the ancestors, cleaning the gravesites, making rituals, eating traditional foods, and burning joss sticks and joss paper. For those who are a bit confused, joss sticks are a type of incense. They are traditionally burned before an Asian religious image, idol,

Buddha statue or shrine. Also, they can be used to make rooms smell better. In the United States calendar, it happened to be around the time of Easter when this event took place in China. I found the parallel to be so educational. Although this occasion occurred on the weekend, Tina still gave us that Friday off in observance.

When moving across the globe, one tends to find things that resemble home. Thankfully with the help of Fred, he introduced me to a small group of people who were Christian. What a gift. One Sunday, he invited me to church and I jumped at the chance. Fred spoke fluent Mandarin and I marveled at that fact. Of course, he lived there for over two years and his wife was Chinese. That made things easier.

Sunday morning around 9:30am, we headed to his friends gathering. It was one thing to see an African American in my city but to spot two of us walking down the street was mayhem. You'd think after almost six months, Asians would get used to seeing me. As we walked inside, he was greeted by a sweet couple. Later, I found out that they were the worship leaders. Downstairs, we passed the kitchen and then were seated in the sanctuary. The hymn was familiar but the words weren't so, I just sang it in English and that was very welcomed. Isn't it amazing that God can understand every language?

After the prayer, they ushered us into a smaller room and the teenagers piled in. They saw me and literally stopped. Fred introduced me and immediately they had several questions about America and Michael Jordan and Michael Jackson! He told them that after class, they could ask their questions.

Fred taught about Job that day and how he was faithful to God regardless of what he lost. He made a point about being grateful no matter what happens to us because we are not meant to stay on this earth. As promised, when class was over, I was bombarded with all things America. They asked me to take a few pictures and I did. We went out to eat at a delicious buffet and then headed to work. That's one more cool experience to add to my memory of all things China!

As June came closer, I kept hearing drums at night. Whether walking home, getting groceries or leaving school, I couldn't tune them out. Little did I know, this expat was in for another treat! The Dragon Boat Festival was approaching. I didn't know what it was, but I couldn't wait to learn. In China, the dragon is paramount. They traditionally symbolize potent and auspicious powers, particularly control over water, rainfall, typhoons, and floods. The dragon is also an emblem of strength and good luck for people who are worthy of it. As you can see, they are a big deal.

Agustin told me that my town of Liushi would be having a grand festival and that we were going. Works for me! Agustin and I were buddies. At his point, he was my best friend in China. We talked every day and laughed all the time. Plus, we were both American and therefore kindred spirits. He too told me that drums were being played at night in his city. Like clockwork, Tina gave us that Friday and Saturday off to enjoy the day.

I guess you are wondering, what exactly is the Dragon Boat Festival, right? Well, let me tell you: During this time of year, historians claim that people believed natural disasters and illnesses were commonplace. In order to get rid of the misfortune, people would put calamus, artemisia, pomegranate flowers, Chinese ixora and garlic above the doors. Since the shape of calamus forms like a sword and with the strong smell of garlic, it is believed that they can remove evil spirits. A highlight of this festival is the Dragon Boat Race. A dragon boat consists of 20 paddlers sitting 2 abreast a cox who steers a dragon boat from the rear and a drummer who sits at the front. The team of paddlers work in unison to propel the boat forward from a standing start, the aim being to reach the finish line in the fastest time. Teams can be male, female, children, old or young! One person has a drum and this sound is to ignite competition and serve as intimidation to the other teams. I was ready!

Friday came and Agustin and I were in place to watch all the races. The colors were so beautiful as each team chose a theme to show unity. Overall, the dragon boat race is to promote community and also religious reasons. Ivy told me that this practice dates back 2,000 years. I saw all my colleagues in the colors of the team they supported. Many of them had family members that they were cheering for in the races. Not only that, the food vendors, merchants and other kiosks lined the streets. Again, being a foreigner has its perks. A vendor gave me a beautiful necklace with a dragon on it in honor of it being my first race. Agustin also received a nice gift. Later that day, we went to a party and a few of the leaders bowed to us! We couldn't believe it! As we were leaving, they presented the two of us with small pouches that were scented. They told us it was for good luck. I often think of this day and Agustin told me he did, too.

As June was coming to an end, Tina asked if I wanted to celebrate my birthday! Are you kidding? Of course I did! Tina needed no excuse to have a party and I supported that. Now, it's one thing to celebrate another year of life, but to do it in ASIA!!! That's freaking amazing! She mentioned if I wanted a theme. Balloons! I told her that I'd love to have tons of balloons and music. The best part about my job was that there was always music playing, usually American. It would not be surprising for my students to come to class and mention the newest American artist they enjoyed. I'd say it might be to curry favor with me, but they genuinely meant it. So, music had to be key on my big day. Tina also suggested champagne because it was a celebration. I told ya - she knew how to throw a party!

July 22nd pushed through on a bright and summery day! Juan picked me up and took me to my favorite spot to eat. We had pizza and French fries! He told the hostess it was my birthday and they brought me the cutest little cake. I destroyed it in three bites. I decided that I would enjoy every single calorie coming my way. After lunch, we went to work. Although Damien was off that day, he still came by to hang out for my party. When I arrived, he was blowing up balloons, placing the silverware, and moving the chairs. Gee, all this for me! Tina had invited the entire school and I was truly humbled.

The guests came in bearing gifts. Laura had arranged an "open mic" of sorts for people to share their experiences with me and how I impacted them. Whoa! I didn't expect that. By nature, Asians are very shy. Therefore, Juan started. This was a good way to get the crowd to warm up and share a few memories. From the first person to the last, each one said I displayed a happy disposition. People are always watching, aren't they? This made me feel good. I have learned that life is short, so you better find the joy in each day. As my party ended, I had Ivy help me carry my new treasures back to our apartment. Many people wanted me to open them there, so I did. From beautiful jewelry to personalized coffee mugs, clothes and unique Chinese keepsakes, I was floored. Thank you, Lord, for another trip around the sun; this one will go down in history.

Bangkok

You've heard the song..."One night in Bangkok!" I had to see if all that I heard was true about this tropical place. So, I got with my colleague and told her to plan my trip to THAILAND!!! It would be an insult having Bangkok so near and not go see her. I was here to teach, but exploring got this expat's blood flowing. I told Tina I needed a week off in August to travel. My fellow foreign teachers had limited passports, so they did not get the opportunities I did to literally go anywhere. An American passport is golden, and I was not going to waste it.

Before I knew it, August was around the corner and I was eager to fly. After conquering Beijing on my own, Bangkok would be no problem. As I checked the weather, my smile grew. Sunny skies were in the forecast and no rain. Could I ask for a better vacation? My suitcase was light because I knew I'd be buying a lot of gifts for family and friends. I spared no expense with my hotel. Let's face it, I was going to be here for seven days and this chick wanted to be comfortable. Americans are willing to pay for one key thing: convenience! My cab arrived around midnight to go to my hotel and the pictures did not do it justice.

<u>I was in Heaven...</u>

Asia Hotel Bangkok was not only beautiful, it was 5-Star! I had the chance to really look and appreciate my surroundings because I was the only one in the lobby. Calling ahead, they were expecting me at the front desk: "Dr. Mose, yes?" "I am she! I replied. After all the paperwork and my passport was reviewed, I was off to my room. Two queen beds, a parlor, huge marble bathroom, desk area, minibar, and refrigerator were all I needed to move in! Here's the thing: Because I had **RMB** currency and then changed it to Thai baht, I tripled my money! I now understood why so many people vacationed in Thailand. You can live like a rockstar due to the money exchange working in your favor. I went to bed that night eager to plan my tours and see what Thailand had in store for this American.

The smell of bacon, eggs and coffee teased my tastebuds. My beloved hotel had a full-course breakfast and I immediately found my seat and went for the carbohydrates. Since I was going to book a private driver, I took my time eating and taking in the scenery: Six buffet bars, a separate omelet spot, beverage station, a live band stage, and pretty people greeted each guest who entered. Gorgeous foliage and a clear sky roof added extra sunshine. I decided that I would dedicate one day on this trip to simply enjoying my hotel.

After I ate, it was time to see Bangkok! Of all the things I had heard about, Wat Pho Museum was first on my list. As I passed the lobby, I saw all the signs for tours and a gentleman behind the desk. We exchanged pleasantries and he showed me all the sites and the best deals. I asked about a personal driver and his reply was, "Pat is the best. He will be here shortly." Roughly 10 minutes later, I met Pat and told him my wishlist. He mentioned it would be "no problem" and asked if I was ready to go immediately. When you travel solo, it's good to know your surroundings. Did I know Pat? No. Did I trust him? Yes. Was there any apprehension of being kidnapped? Yep, sure was! The good thing is that Pat and I were able to communicate well with each other and establish mutual respect early. I mentioned that I was an American and he said, "I love President Obama!" In life, you gotta trust your gut and simply go for it. This small piece of advice has broadened my life in countless ways.

The Reclining Buddha...I had to see it. After all, not only it is infamous, it just seems unreal. Pat and I headed to Wat Pho Museum and I explained to him my love of pictures. Due to dealing with tons of tourists, he knew the drill. Wat Pho is a Buddhist temple. It's located in the Phra Nakhon District in Bangkok. It actually sits on an island. The temple complex houses the largest collection of Buddha images in Thailand! The other unique thing I read is that it houses a school of Thai medicine. It's considered the birthplace of traditional Thai massage, which is still taught and practiced in the temple to this day.

As we approached the temple, there were several tourists. The weather was beautiful and there were so many signs to read. I did not know that you were not supposed to touch the monks. Also, the sign mentioned no illegal tampering with the artifacts and to always use respect. It's a shame they had to say this, but I get it. Not everyone sees other cultures as important or necessary. This is part of why I wanted to see the beauty of this country.

Thanks to Pat, I wore shoes that were easy to get in and out of for our trip. Shoes were not allowed in any of the temples. We went to the Reclining Buddha first. The line was long but moved rather quickly. The many security guards were big in stature, yet smiled at everyone. I looked to my left and there it was. Pat gave me a pail and then he told me to buy pennies. As we kept walking inside, to the right was a long line of pails mounted against the wall in a row, and you had the option of dropping pennies, dollars or any currency towards the upkeep of the temple. Some people chose not to do this, but I eagerly participated. When we finished the long line of pennies, we got in another line to take a picture with one of the MOST FAMOUS Buddhas in the world. My long time editor told me that "pictures are proof." She was right: if you really see the cool stuff, there should be some tangible evidence. I got it alright in spades.

It was my turn and I was a kid in a candy store. First the Great Wall of China in Beijing and now the Reclining Buddha here Bangkok. It is one thing to see these sites in books; it is something altogether different to see them up close and personal. As I looked at the Reclining Buddha, I saw this large panel over its head. Pat told me that is was a nine-tiered umbrella and it represented the authority of Thailand. Amazing...

We walked more and more into the museum and my eyes were blessed. So many Buddhas and what a time to witness this. Many times, I turned around and looked at where I was standing. Denise Mose was NOT in the USA. I was NOT in China. I was here. My arms were getting tired of being pinched; I had to find a new spot. Several pictures were taken that morning and Pat enjoyed seeing this through my eyes. Three hours later, we got back into his car and I didn't see it before, but I did now: He had a mini Buddha on his console and he said it gave him good luck while he was on the road.

Later that day, he took me to a wonderful lunch and we rode all over the city. Elephants are everywhere in Bangkok, including on the royal Thai Navy flag. Historically, elephants in Thailand are considered very important culturally. White elephants in Thai society represent wealth and power because of their past association with the Thai royals. Also, they are admired for their strength, mental faculties, cooperative spirit and loyalty. Sculptures, statues, paintings, murals, t-shirts and everything else that could be sold had the face of an elephant.

After the museum and lunch, Pat took me for a massage. He parked and I really did not know what was in store for me. Two ladies welcomed us with tea that had pretty flowers in the cup. I looked at Pat and took my cup. My mind said, "When in Rome!" I said a prayer and drank the liquid sans the flowers. That was some of the best tea I'd ever had, bar none. Pat later told me that the flowers were hibiscus and good for reducing blood pressure. Also, they smelled divine.

They directed us to a private room and gave us these beautiful gowns to put on. I went into the women's bathroom and he changed clothes in the men's room. Pat was my eyes through all of this, and I trusted him; this he knew. After we put on the silk pajamas, they brought us a tray of exotic fruit, the kinds of which I had never seen. Again, I spoke to Jesus and began eating. Here in the Far East, food is sacred. They do not waste it, and it shows. The massage was perfect, and I had no idea that it was nearly dark outside. With that, we headed back to the hotel. The next day would be a tour of the Floating Market and I was going to have my ride through the jungle on an elephant! I couldn't wait.

I met Pat at 8am in the lobby because he said the events for today were not close. Therefore, a long roadtrip was on our agenda, but not without a coffee stop at Starbucks. I was going to do it folks: Ride an elephant in the jungle!!! Talk about your bucket list! After an hour of driving, we turned into a side street and then it opened into a big park. We saw a few tourists and the ticket booth. I have learned that when you go to a foreign place, do yourself a favor and secure a local who knows how to help you. They can navigate the language and often cut you a great deal on sites to see without being taken advantage of because you don't know any better.

Pat gave me my ticket and waited for me at the exit. They ushered me to a huge ladder and that's when it hit me why I had to climb so high. I ascended the steps because I would be getting on the elephant from this height. As guests got off, I saw the elephants. My goodness, they were brobdingnagian!!! This was my first time seeing one up close and I was certainly a novice at touching such a creature. The guide held my hand and told me to gently sit on the seat and prepare for a great time. Furthermore, he encouraged me to take lots of pictures. Pat took many snapshots of me, too. There was no belt to hold onto, just a sliver bar in front for balance. My guide explained the jungle and that elephants, by nature, are very friendly. Awe...I was in total awe. Denise Yvette Mose of Huntsville, Alabama, was riding an elephant in Bangkok, Thailand. A tear shed my eye because I wanted to share this moment with my mom. I rested in the fact that she was close by and smiling at me.

Forty minutes later, I was on the ground. The tour guide told me to come toward the front, so I could look at the elephant. Then, he instructed me to turn around so that my back was to it. A secret laugh between Pat and my guide told me they were up to something. The guide asked me to move closer to the elephant and hold out my hands. Scared, psyched and worried - I obeyed. Before I knew it, my feet were hoisted off the ground and the elephant's trunk was around my waist. WHAT? Laughter took over and it was a picture worth a thousand words. Not exactly sure how you can top being picked up by an elephant in the jungle while vacationing in Bangkok, but hey - I had a few more days to go! We went into the gift shop and I purchased some mementos. Of course, I bought any and everything that had an elephant on it.

Pat told me that we were on our way to THE FLOATING MARKET!!! Ahhh! Yes! I saw pictures of this and knew that my trip would be incomplete if we didn't go. It wasn't that far from the jungle ride so that was helpful. Pat parked his car and got my ticket. He said it takes two hours to see everything by boat and that he would wait for me. One of the drivers showed me his boat and we were headed down the river. Once you get in the boat, you don't see anything except for a few houses. As we made the first turn, I heard voices and then there they were...

So...many...boats...

Boats with everything and anything you could ever want. In my lifetime, I had never seen such a marvel. Each boat had a vendor (at eye level) who was selling their wares. Clothes, fruit, drinks, and souvenirs were at your disposal. When I tell you that I saw people with an actual stove on their boat, that is exactly what I mean. Hot and ready meals were made in front of you...for a small fee, of course. It was literally a floating kitchen. I was told that we were at the Damnoen Floating Market and this one was the most popular. This is a bygone way of life for the locals and I just sat in wonder at what my eyes were seeing.

How do you sell everything from a boat? The beauty was that we could barter on any goods they had. Furthermore, there were stand-alone shops right next to the water. I see how this makes things convenient to the seller. Just then, a boat passed and she had so many Chinese trinkets that I knew she would get my money. She had the Emperor Boading Balls and in so many colors. I knew I was going to purchase more for family and friends. As she wrapped up my gifts, the driver sped up the boat and we went to check out more stuff.

My driver really let me take this in. He was pleasant and clearly used to many of my kind: tourists. We rode, and I was shocked at how two hours flew by. Pat was waiting for me as I exited the boat. My hands full of goodies, he assisted me back to the car.

Back at the hotel, I ordered room service. After being picked up by an elephant and seeing the historic Floating Market, my mind was in overdrive. My only proof was the bevy of pictures I took on my iPhone. There was a knock on the door and my tummy rumbled in anticipation of dinner. I could smell the bacon cheeseburger, French fries and Coca-Cola making their way towards me. A banana split helped me finish off my epic day. Pat reminded me to rest again because the next day, a tiger was in my future...Thailand was giving me my BEST LIFE!

YOLO (You Only Live Once) is a popular saying. Pat told me that today would be another unforgettable 24 hours in Thailand. Given our history, I believed him. Again, we grabbed coffee and drove at least an hour towards my next adventure. I had heard of the Tiger Temple in Thailand. I mean, there are quite a few of them, but this one in particular was the best one to see. Honestly, I really wanted to see how the monks interacted with the tigers. Pat told me that the tigers are raised as babies within this temple. Therefore, there is a familiar relationship between man and animal. We arrived at the temple and parked the car. Pat paid our fee and we walked toward the entrance with our guide.

As we walked down the hill, I felt so much peace. It was a large enclosure and obviously sat on several acres. We arrived at the tourist area and there they were...TIGERS. They ranged from Full-grown adults to babies. A few people were actually feeding the baby tigers milk and it was absolutely precious. Pat spoke to a few of the trainers to allow me to get my picture and possibly "walk" a tiger a bit. YOLO, right? After all, did I really venture this far just to look, or to ascertain a once-in-a-lifetime moment? Exactly, I went for it!

After the tourist in front of me was done, I told the guide I was ready. He directed me where to stand and reminded me to stay still. Slowly, he asked (yes, asked), the tiger to crouch down and be good. WHAT??? In my head, I said the following, "It will be over before you know it, Denise!" Carefully, I moved behind the tiger and lowered myself. He instructed me to put my hand on the back part of the tiger, which I did. Once Pat started taking the pictures, the guide told me to rise and walk to my right. He moved the tiger to the next tourist. WHEW!!!!! I did it! I actually did it! At least six monks were sitting near all of the tigers. They only carried a walking stick and seemed very pleasant. Pat mentioned the monks were not to be touched by anyone, especially tourists. I did my best not to stare, so I snuck a few looks and simply smiled. I met several other tourists that day and we were all pretty psyched about hanging out with a tiger. Talk about a memory.

On the way back, we stopped at a popular place. It was a high Black Bridge and it was truly crowded. Pat said I had to walk on the bridge and take a lot of pictures. So, being an authentic American, I included the folks on the bridge with me and took many photos. Before we jumped back in the car, Mother Nature called so I was in search of a restroom. We parked at a convenience store with a bathroom adjacent. A sweet older lady was nearby, so I spoke to her. As I pushed the door to enter, it did not open. Again, I pressed on the door for entry and nothing happened. Very kindly, she held out her hand. I was confused. As if on cue, Pat appeared. He said, "Denise, you have to pay to use the restroom." Shock was all I could muster. Pay? Pay to use the restroom? I looked at her and her hand had not changed. It was then that I saw the sign for payment. I produced the amount to use the restroom and she unlocked the door. For as long as I live, I will remember her face. She was very sweet and meant business. I laughed to myself as we headed back. Another wonderful lesson about traveling!

After my shower and as the evening rolled around, I prepared for the night's entertainment. You cannot visit Thailand without seeing a "Drag Queen" show. Thankfully, my resort had one on the first floor. I sat up front and was eager to see what the fuss was about. Well, now I know. Every famous performer was represented on that stage. WOW! They could sing, dance and they embodied their character. Two hours later, I was floored. Afterwards, I took pictures with the "queens," but this tourist didn't realize that they expected payment for the picture. Uh oh! This is why it is good to travel. They made their money from tips. Since my room was upstairs, I had no need to carry a lot of cash on me. Therefore, I made my exit rather quickly and headed to the nearest elevator. Lesson learned!

Sleep, sleep and more sleep. I had one thing planned for this day and that didn't happen until later in the evening. Ergo, I decided to ease into my day and enjoy my resort. The Asia Hotel Bangkok was NICE! Here's the thing: Bangkok is a beautiful place to visit and extremely affordable. This was a 5-Star hotel and I thoroughly spoiled myself.

The pool! Big, blue and beautiful. That's the only way for me to describe it. I knew where I would be spending this day. A very handsome bartender walked over to me and asked what I'd like to drink. You guessed it, I ordered a mimosa. I figured it was right on time for brunch, so I got the classic libation. The towels were available and so were courtesy flip flops. I was in Heaven. Fresh fruit, sunshine, peace and an exotic country made this the perfect day for me. Three hours later and I was back in my room. I showered and headed to the Asian restaurant because the food had been teasing me since I arrived. Egg rolls, tasty fried rice, orange chicken, sticky ribs, grilled vegetables and more yummy stuff filled my belly. Once I paid the bill, my bed was calling me. A much-needed nap was up next.

Around 3:30pm, I checked out the spa. Scents of lavender and jasmine summoned my nostrils as I entered. Three nice ladies asked me what I'd like to have done and of course, champagne was offered. Thailand is the best!!! I chose the massage that spoke to me and then they gave me a very pretty silk pajama set. When I tell you it was hypnotizing, that's exactly what I mean. Truthfully, massages were basically invented in the Far East; these folks are the experts. Tension relief, muscles soothed, flexibility increased, and overall renewed energy was what I walked away with.

A familiar knock on my door let me know that my taste buds would soon be happy. A medium rare steak, baked potato, salad, roll, cheesecake, ice cream and red wine made their way to my room. I found a good movie and treated myself. Realizing that I was going to miss my evening show, I called Pat and he made plans for tomorrow. My movie ended and I put my food in the hallway. I was knocked out in minutes.

SIAM NIRAMIT DINNER SHOW! I do not know where to begin. The majesty, history, colors, sounds, costumes, music, animals and the feeling. My last night in Thailand was one for the record books. In the morning, I shopped until I dropped, and I did the show at night. No one was omitted in my quest to find the coolest trinkets for my loved ones back home. I purchased a dinkum outfit to wear to the dinner show later. Pat told me that this was the most attended live show in Thailand, and it showcased a lot about this tropical country. He didn't lie either.

We arrived at the show and ate first. I've seen big dining halls, but this was astronomical! Pat took our tickets and the host seated us. Then, something hit me: I was going to miss Pat. After all, we had been together for seven days and I owe one of my best vacations to his hospitality. The food was incredible and terribly delicious. Although we ordered tea, wine was served to everyone. The hostess came by and mentioned that the outside show was beginning. Outside show? Pat said that we had to get our seats. Following the crowd, there was an open area clearly prepared for a performance. Before I knew it, an elephant and his trainer strolled through the center of the audience. Music played and people came out of nowhere. I snapped so many photos, intent on not missing any details.

The Siam Niramit compound showed a lot of the Thai culture. Once the show was over, we had time to look around, see the shops, and talk to tour guides and the performers. I kept seeing a sculpture of Kinnaree, a mythical winged creature prevalent in many Thai fables. Further in, there was a lady making Thai treats and sewing various outfits. I sat and watched how she so effortlessly made beautiful outfits in no time at all. Pat told me that many of these customs had been passed down from 700 years of tradition. Thailand spans seven centuries!

The show began and my eyes refused to blink. Stage production was on the level of the Academy Awards! The ladies with the long gold nails and the beautiful headpieces blew me away. The belly dancers asked the audience to participate and I knew this was not for me. Flying acrobats, smoke, creatures and back-defying dancers entertained everyone for well over 90 minutes. Pat and I sat there in wonder. Thailand is an intriguing Asian nation. I'll definitely be back.

Checking out of my hotel was painful. Geez, I'd been here a whole week. Pat drove me to the airport and that was where we embraced. Boarding my flight and finding my seat had me in a trance. As much as I enjoyed my job, it was good for me to see the other countries near Asia - So glad that I did.

Moment to Pause...Mid-Autumn Festival

I need to breathe a bit. By now, I had been in China for over six months. The saying is really true: "Time flies when you are having fun." From not knowing anyone over here to having a kaleidoscope of friends was my reality. Nouchelle and I laugh about how all of this came to fruition. What began as a joke ended up with me moving to another continent and finding out so much more about myself. Life is a funny thing. Risk and reward go hand in hand. I am better because of this entire sojourn.

As September rolled around, so did another festival. I was grateful to learn about Asia and its many holidays that were observed. The Mid-Autumn Festival begins around September 13th to 15th of each year. The Mid-Autumn Festival is the second grandest celebration in China after Chinese New Year. The name comes from always being honored in the middle of autumn season. You might also hear og Moon Festival. This is the time of year when the moon is at its roundest and brightest.

Mid-Autumn Festival is an inherited custom of moon and sacrificial ceremonies. The ancient Chinese observed that the movement of the moon had a close relationship with changes of the seasons and agricultural production. Hence, this festival expresses their thanks to the moon and pays homage for the harvest. People in mainland China enjoy one day off on the festival which is usually connected with the weekend. In Hong Kong and Macau, people also enjoy a day of no labor. In Taiwan, it's the same.

Sweet cakes, pastries and good food is what I remembered most on this special occasion. In fact, the cakes are called moon cakes. My students gave me many cakes on this day. Family members expressed their yearning toward other relatives who were far away. Other traditions included dragon and lion dances in various regions.

The day came to an end and Tina mentioned a few more dates to us. I was itching to plan my next trip and I knew where it would be...

Shanghai

Tina informed us that during October, there would be a three-day break. Apparently, a celebration known as "National Day" was to be celebrated. Cool, I thought. A few of the foreign teachers made a list of where we wanted to go and narrowed it down. We only had three days, so we needed some place close. The decision was made: SHANGHAI. Yes! I had heard that it was called "The New York" of China. Well, this I had to see.

We were only four hours away by train and that made me very happy. Seeing China by train was literally the most calming thing in the world. I got with my good friend Lis, and he booked my ticket. The best part about currency exchange is the value. Since I saved a good portion of my pay, a first-class ticket would be right up my alley. Peter, Damon and Juan also joined me by train. We were like family. After all, I saw them every day and we planned the class assignments together.

Arriving in Shanghai was a madhouse. We stepped off the train and looked for a taxi to our hotel. The guys stayed a little further out of town, and I chose to stay in the city. Because I like convenience, my hotel was near many of the major sites, so I could easily walk or grab a cab to where I wanted to go. There was no Uber or Lyft at this time; if so, I would've used that. My hit list was made of the key things I had to do and see. Being American, I'm used to traveling solo. I couldn't wait on the guys; I hit the road early.

Oriental Pearl TV Tower: This is one of the tallest towers in Shanghai. The color alone makes it interesting. Reading the reports online told me I should get my ticket early and get in line. Boy, were they right. Although I showed up early, I still had to wait a good hour. That beats the four-hour torture that some people had to endure later that day. Like any good attraction, there was a souvenir shop on your way in to entice all to buy many gifts. I penciled this in on my way out. Finally, I made my way to the elevator and from there, the guide took you to the level that you wanted. The top level was for a special dinner and that you had to pay an extra fee for. I didn't need that – my goal was the clear floor. Being elevated at roughly 1,000 feet in the air was on my bucket list! Many people can't handle this, but I could. Carpe Diem!!!

Ok, it's one thing to see this on television, it is entirely different when your feet are touching a glass floor and you are looking straight down. Whoa! This was creepy yet thrilling. Immediately, I pulled out my iPhone and started snapping. Also, a photographer was there to capture tourist in funny poses – obviously, I obliged. Two hours later after circling the entire glass floor, I headed back downstairs. Several gifts were purchased for my family and friends from the shop. As the sun hit me when I got outside, the line had swarmed even more. It pays to be early.

Shanghai Disney: The sad part is that right as I was ending my journey in China, this amazing feat was opening! Can you believe that? So, unfortunately, I have no news to report on this site. However, give me two years. I'll discuss it then.

Shanghai World Financial Center: Breathtaking, mind-bending, architectural wonder, and silver. I could go on and on, but I'll stop at those adjectives. The Shanghai World Financial Center ("SWFC") is located in the Pudong district of this beautiful city. It is an astronomical skyscraper and several things happen in this enticing edifice. Offices, hotels, conference rooms, restaurants, observation decks, and ground-floor shopping malls all reside here. You see this building from miles away; in fact, my tour guide said it was an architecture type called neo-futurism. Completed in 2008, it cost well over one billion dollars. I have to say this: China is a country that means to impress each and every person who visits. I've run out of things to say about its landscape and the sheer beauty of its waterfalls. Why would their skyscrapers be any different? The coolest part of the SWFC is the top – A trapezoid aperture is at its peak. When you ascend the elevator, you will notice three observation decks. I won't go into further detail; you'll just have to see it for yourself but be sure to go. Another awesome feature is seeing this at night. The lights illuminate in such a way that you don't want to blink in case you miss something.

Longhua Temple: So much history is in Shanghai and it was my goal to see as much as I could. Next on my list was one of its most revered temples. Longhua is a Buddhist temple dedicated to the Maitreya Buddha in Shanghai. This temple preserves the architectural design of the Song Dynasty Monastery of the Chan School. It is the largest, most authentic and complete ancient temple complex in the city of Shanghai. Pictures do not give the temple justice. Heart-stopping is a better way to describe how I was feeling. There are small gardens that absorb the cemetery nearby. Tranquil is the word that applies here. Also, there are several signs that warn against taking pictures inside the temple. Traveling is its own education. I've said that many times, especially this book. Yet, it bears repeating. Despite how much you may want to do something on another continent or in a certain country; there are rules to follow. Please make sure you do that.

There are over 500 arhats in this temple. An arhat is a Buddhist who has reached the stage of enlightenment. Representatives are all over the temple and you must not take their photo. The eye-catching feature that everyone notices is the 16 historic padogas that still stand within the Shanghai municipality. The octagonal floor layout gives way to the seven stories of this temple. On the outside, it is decorated with balconies, banisters, and upturned eaves. Because it is so fragile, it is not open to the public. When in Shanghai, add it to your list.

Nanjing Road: Another spot on my trip to Shanghai was this famous road. I was told if you want to buy any and everything, this was where you had to go. Nanjing Road is the main shopping street in Shanghai and one of the busiest streets in the world. Before you enter the street, a sign explains how the name was formed. Najing is the capitol of Jiangsu, neighboring Shanghai. Today's Nanjing Road comprises two sections: East and West. The part I explored was mostly East. It is more developed with so many shops, beautiful restaurants, and incredible people. Again, because we were traveling by train, I did not have a big issue with too many bags. If I were flying, that would be a different story. Later on that day, I found my fellow cohorts. Peter, Juan and Damon were all walking towards me and hunger was on our agenda. On our last night in Shanghai, we grabbed a scrumptious dinner, walked around the city and took an iconic picture in front of the Pear Tower. Ahhh! What a special trip.

We returned to work on the following Monday and Tina had another surprise for us! Little did we know that another party was just around the corner. Since we were already in the month of October, it made my mind wander. Halloween! I bet we were going to have a soiree. I mean, Tina loved to party and really didn't need a reason. Americans love to celebrate, and Halloween is a popular day that we embrace whole-heartedly. As we had our weekly staff meeting, she passed out the flyer for out next event. Yep! A party with all things that relate to Halloween. I've learned that part of the Asian culture lies in mythical creatures and what day has more fantasied stories than the last day in October? Tina encouraged us to dress up and she would even pay for the costumes. I knew which character I wanted to be for the party...

STORM from X-MEN! Now, Americans know who she is but for those that don't, allow me to educate you for a moment. Storm is fictional superhero who appeared in American comic books in 1975. She is the first Black female hero. She has superhuman abilities that came to her at birth. She is known as a mutant. Storm can control the weather and atmosphere. The X-Men are a team of superheroes written by Stan Lee and Jack Kirby. The X-Men fight for peace and equality with non-mutants who threaten their way of life. Professor Charles Xavier, a powerful mutant telepath who can control and reads minds, is the fearless leader of this group. Now, does that help? Good, back to Halloween in China.

Saturday was the big day and we had been preparing all week. Tina ordered the food, drinks, games and champagne. First of all, when we had our first party there was alcohol. This is not surprising for an after-hours party in America to serve alcohol; in fact, it's a social standard. However, I did not know that this was also done in China. I felt better after my first party when Tina brought me a glass of white wine. I mean, if the boss is bringing you alcohol, it would be rude to refuse, right? That's what I thought.

Balloons, streamers, desks rearranged, pretty tablecloths, lots of food and Michael Jackson's "Thriller" on repeat. WOW! This was going to be a huge night. Agustin, Juan, Damon, Ethan (new friend) and a few other fellow foreign teachers dropped by to dance the night away. Tina also had plenty of games for the evening festivities. The best part was many of the guests shared a few Asian Folklore stories and it was so powerful. I would have never known about any of these legendary tales had I not spent this monumental year abroad in Asia.

The party was a blast and we decided to keep it going. Several of us went to a popular restaurant and ordered pizza, burgers, fries and Coca-Cola. Very American, right? What can I say? I have totally influenced my new friends. We had such a fun night and it will go down in history.

Little did I know, another party was just a few weeks away.

Thanksgiving

It is fitting that this celebrated holiday comes at the end of the year - That way, one must really contemplate how thankful the entire year has been to them. Geez, I remember getting my work visa for China and now Thanksgiving was upon us. Time truly flies when you are having fun.

Tina knew all the Western traditions that coincided with Thanksgiving, yet she still came to me with ideas for another party. Through the beauty of social media, I posted everyday what my adventures were. To some, it seemed like there was a party every minute. The crazy thing about this whole experience is that I was having the time of my life. So yeah, it probably did look like complete jubilation at every turn. I had a boss who loved to honor traditions and she had an American who shared those values. But Tina and I didn't start out so chummy...

My first day at George English Training School involved a lot of orientation, finding my way, learning the system and creating my comfort level. We were on the fourth floor. Tina was the one who picked me up from the airport and was my liaison. Laura trained me on our nightly "English Corner" and told me that I had autonomy on the topics. Great! Americans really are not huge fans of a micro-management workplace. Do they exist? Of course - it's just not something I had experienced...until now.

Around my third week at the school, I was preparing a lesson on "Greetings" and Tina mentioned that she wanted to see my PowerPoint presentation. Cool, this suited me just fine. She came and sat beside me as I was about to explain the slides. Immediately, she told me to change my colors, fonts, style and use more slides. Stumped...I was stumped.

Laura was there to translate and serve as a "buffer" between us. I asked Tina to allow me to finish my PPT first and then I'd love to hear her comments. That didn't happen. Her voice was raised, and she began to point at me. Oh, Jesus!

I looked at Laura and my eyes told her exactly how I was feeling towards this behavior from Tina. Laura tried to talk to Tina, but she was not having it. Then, she said she would do a lesson and for me to use her example.

Nope, no way. As a professional educator with over 15 years at every level of education, I was not going to put up with this. I was asked to teach here by Mr. Frank Sun, my interviewer, and boy was my phone ready to dial his number. Tina continued to yell and point, so I simply stood up and walked away. I told Laura that I needed some fresh air.

Juan and a few other colleagues came to the bathroom where I was doing my best to calm down. Immediately, Juan hugged me. He's Western, he knows. Many of them asked if I was ok. Clearly, I was not. I'll be forever grateful to them for understanding body language. No matter where you are in the world, if someone is upset, you don't need words to define what's happening. From what Juan told me, I did not know that I was raising my voice - that's how upset I was.

I had to assess the situation. Here's what my mind was thinking: One, I was on a different continent. Two, I signed a contract. Three, I just started this job. Four, none of the food was familiar. Five, I wanted my dad and to cry my eyes out. Six, I had to remain professional - get it together, Denise! Seven, my colleagues were looking at how I was going to handle this and being a good example was important to me.

I counted to 10 and when my eyes were opened, Tina was there. She looked very sorrowful and offered a very sincere apology. I did the same. I explained to her that her style of supervising was a serious problem for me. Micro-management is not an effective practice and belittles your staff. Tina mentioned that this was her preferred way of keeping a tight staff. Laura explained that this was very prominent in most authentic Asian companies. Tina told me that she had never worked with an American before and didn't realize that we (me) were so vocal in everything. Oh, yes, lady, I'm a true American! Before long, we were able to laugh and joke about this whole situation. Juan stayed with me the entire time and eventually I finished my PPT. Class was great that night and you'd never know fireworks exploded a mere few hours before they arrived.

I'm thankful that I held my composure while talking to my boss. It is key to have folks around you who are different - it helps you grow. Tina and I did not get along that day, but we had to find a common ground. The truth is this: she needed me and I needed her. That problem could have had a very different outcome. I'm grateful it didn't. Tina and I still email to this day.

Wine, champagne, beer, potatoes, chips, crabs, shrimp, delicious vegetables and one of the biggest turkeys I'd ever seen in my life made the perfect Thanksgiving spread! I must say, Tina spares no expense when it comes to having a good time. Whenever we had parties, the School staff and their families were always invited. As my journey was coming to an end, it seemed like that's what we truly were now: Family.

Christmas in Dubai

Tokyo, Singapore and Dubai. I knew there would be one last "hoorah" before I left to go home for good. Weighing my options was important because I really did not know when I'd be on this end of the world again. Therefore, I had to "go out with a bang" on this last trek. After talking to Danny, John, Danielle, Monique, Nouchelle, Juan, Agustin and my dad, it was unanimous: DUBAI!!!

Tina informed us of the days that we would be getting off for Christmas. I submitted three extra days to simply take in all of Dubai. A full seven days should cover my time in this bubbling city. Up until about 10 years ago, I had not heard much of Dubai. However, with its tourist attractions, cleanliness, extravagance, and growing popularity, I'd be crazy not to go.

I was all set for my week in Dubai and suddenly found myself very sad. This was my last big trip - Beijing, Hangzhou, Guangzhou, Ningbo, Yeuqing, Wenzhou, Suzhou, Nanjing, Xiamen, Shenzen, Hong Kong, Bangkok, Shanghai and now Dubai. I had explored so many places on my days off, too. When you meet me at my book signing, I'll discuss some of the places not gone into detail here. I can't put everything in my book, y'all!

As we landed in Dubai, I, of course, had to go through customs. This is such a powerful experience when you travel because patience is critical. Because its Dubai, there are several long lines. However, it is extremely efficient, and you won't be there long. The first thing I noticed were the customs agents. They were all in long white Thawbs (kandoora or dishdasha) garments. There are other names, depending on where you are coming from. On their heads were Mustahabbs. I learned that those who believed in the prophet Muhammad, covered their heads in honor to him. It's one thing to see this on television but live and up close - spellbinding!

My turn arrived and I waited for them to make eye contact. I smiled and presented my passport. The agent was extremely handsome and well-groomed. He looked thoroughly in my passport and was clearly shocked to see that I was a teacher from China. Furthermore, he noticed all of the stamps of the other places I had visited. After keeping my passport for well over three minutes, he inquired about my visit. I told him that my fellow foreign teachers were working in his city and had invited me. His hand gestures motioned for me to give more detail, so I told him they were also African American and female. The questions stopped then. My passport was returned with a stamp and I was off to get my cab.

I knew that if I found the right driver and told them what I wanted to do in the city, they would be with me all week...for the right price, of course. Bearing that in mind, I looked carefully at body language, vehicles, language pronunciation and weight when picking my driver. Let's be honest: a female traveling alone, small stature and slim can sometimes be a target. This is true no matter what place you visit. So, I made sure that I took good care of Denise.

A nice tall man who wasn't overly eager to get my business asked if I needed a ride. His vehicle was a silver Mercedes Benz and very clean. I prayed to myself and told him the address of my hotel. He gave me a great smile and then asked what I wanted to explore in Dubai. Well, I mentioned the main sites and casually said that I could use a personal driver. Quickly he offered, we discussed payment and Aadil said he'd be with me all week. Done!

Holiday Inn Express Dubai would be my home for the next seven days. The best part was the full breakfast, business center and I was near everything. Furthermore, a few of the sites were not admissible by car. So, the hotel was able to book them for me. My room was just what I wanted: Two queen beds! One for me and one for my clothes! After a shower, I contacted Dr. Danielle Ardella Mincey. She was a foreign professor teaching in Dubai and a mutual friend of my "Big Sister" Yvette Register!

Food - the first thing we did was get some grub. Little did I know, not far from my hotel was one of the many malls in Dubai. Dr. Danielle and I smelled the French fries a mile away. However, since she is a devout vegetarian, we agreed on a happy medium. It was so cool to meet a fellow Black foreign teacher who was doing her "thang" in Dubai. Let me just say, that was some cool "Black Girl

Magic!" For those unfamiliar with that term, you won't be for long. Simply ask any millennial and they will tell you. The restaurant was bustling with tourists and since I didn't want to miss anything, we sat outside. It was a comfortable night and the breeze was perfect. She drove me all over the highway and my mind was in wonderland. Dubai was simply beautiful and even that word doesn't do it justice. I went to bed that night thanking the Lord for such a time as this...

Burj Khalifa: Whoa! That's pretty much my only word for this skyscraper. It is the tallest structure and building in the entire world. Like any iconic edifice, its got a line out the door to go inside. Thankfully, my awesome tour guide arranged all of that when I mentioned the key things I wanted to see. The best view is the observation deck on the 124th floor. The clear floor is another "can't miss" item. I mean, what more proof do you need to know you are up so high? On another note, when movie star Tom Cruise filmed *Mission Impossible -- Ghost Patrol*, he did some of his most iconic stunts at this building. You want to be legendary? Have a Hollywood Star feature your hotel in their movie. If it wasn't already famous, the Burj Khalifa became so after the movie was released. Oh! Be sure to catch the water show in the evening.

Burj Al Arab Jumeirah: Look! Please forgive me for saying this - Some of the most jaw-dropping sites I have had the pleasure of seeing with my two eyes are in the Far East. The Burj Al Arab Jumeirah has a sail-shaped silhouette and serves as a beacon for all who visit Dubai. In recent years, it has been voted as one of (if not THE) most luxurious hotel in the world. When your hotel can boast having nine world-class restaurants, I think you are in a class all your own. After all, you can choose to have a Rolls Royce serve as your chauffeur. Aadil took me on the private beach and it was so pretty. Even the sand was dazzling. I ordered a drink so that I looked like I was a regular. I tell ya, it's who you know, right? Aadil took my picture and we went to the next site.

Desert Safari and Dinner Show: "Don't be a punk, Denise!" This is what I told myself repeatedly as we rode to the Desert Safari Tour. I saw the pictures, heard all the rumors and booked it anyway. Did I come this far to NOT do it? No! After all, I had a solid will and my attorney knew my wishes. In the worst-case scenario, my heirs were well-informed should I have an untimely demise in the desert in Dubai. I made sure not to eat before the ride because I figured I would surely see it again. Aadil was with me the whole time. This tour consisted of the Desert Tour and then the Dinner Show. I prayed I lived through it. He mentioned that we would be in a large Hummer and to expect the "best ride of my life." Seven people got in the Hummer and it started off rather slow. He played some light music and told us that if anyone felt sick to let him know. I saw the many sand dunes and wondered to myself how we would get across the entire desert. Suddenly, we were diving down a sand dune and boy did it go on forever. Not only that, the tires were sliding, and I swore I saw my life flash before my eyes.

Screaming, shouting, laughter, tears and hysteria surrounded me. A little girl and I were the only consistent siren calls that the driver heard. I realized I was making things worse by actually looking out at what was coming next. Closing my eyes, breathing slowly and silently praying got me through the next 30 minutes. When we finally got out of the Hummer, I actually fell over and stayed on the ground for a while. Getting my bearings was my first priority. My night wasn't over, there was a camel in my near future. Aadil walked me over to the camels and quickly showed me how to get on one graciously. That didn't work, I nearly fell. If you've never ridden a camel, here is one thing to know: you will truly be high off the ground. Yes, I reckon that's rather obvious, but it is quite different when you are on one. The scary part was getting off the camel; they get very low to the point that falling seems like a good idea. Whew! That's two more things taken off my Dubai Bucket List.

Here comes the third: Dinner in the Desert. After jumping the sand dunes in the Hummer and my camel experience, it was time to eat. Thankfully, food was near. However, dinner wasn't quite ready, so I visited the boutiques nearby and had an idea: Henna. The beautiful ladies were drawing Henna on the tourists and I was not going to miss out. I chose my design and sat down. I tell ya, this was a very cool surprise. The lady was very nice and asked me many questions. Because I was Black, several of the other tourist thought that I was Jamaican, African or Cuban. This never offended me, it just showed me how limited some people's thinking really seemed to be. President Barack Obama held the highest office in the United States - Was it really so hard to believe that I was a US Citizen? Anyway, she immediately told me that she wanted to visit my country and see New York City. Well, who doesn't?

Soon, the buffet was ready, and it was perfect. Everything you could think of was served. Of course, having so many tourists, you had to meet the needs of a very diverse crowd. I found my seat and sat right in front where the Belly Dancer was going to perform. Two hours later and my mouth was still open. This day was one for the books. Returning to my hotel that night I looked at my hand covered in beautiful Henna. A perfect memory for an astounding day. I still had four more days to go and they were just as packed as this one.

The Grand Mosque: I had to see this. If you visit Dubai and don't see the Grand Mosque, did you even go? Aadil told me that if I wanted to go inside the Mosque, I had to wear a Burqa. This excited me. I was always curious about what a Burqa felt like. Were they heavy? Did it have pockets? Would it be too long? I had so many questions – yet I couldn't wait. Aadil picked me up at around 7:45 in the morning because the Grand Mosque is located in Abu Dhabi. This is roughly 90 minutes outside of Dubai and serves as the capital of The United Arab Emirates (UAE). Folks, Dubai is perfect; Abu Dhabi is spotless. Yes, they are both synonymous to the other and that's exactly what I meant. If you haven't been, you must go. Anyway, back to the Grand Mosque.

As you approach the Mosque, it doesn't seem real. It is like something out of a dream. I read that it was based off the Sultan's home in the 1992 Disney Movie Aladdin. I saw the movie recently and it brought back these memories of my time in Dubai. There were several signs outside about not touching anything and following the rules. After all, I was in a Muslim country. I made sure to respect the rules and my demeanor at all times. Aadil took me to a room where there were designated lines for men and women. Anyone who wished to go in the Mosque had to surrender their passport in exchange for a Burqa. Because I had traveled so much, this was nothing new. I was a foreigner and many people were looking for any reason to stay in certain countries. Aadil pointed me in the right line. I surrendered my passport, was fitted for a Burqa, signed my name and off I went. We went up the escalator and found the incredible entrance. Pearl, gold, platinum, emeralds and rubies were there for you to salivate. The rugs were real Persian and the stunning chandeliers made you look twice. My iPhone had plenty of storage for the pictures I was taking. I love taking photos because it's an authentic memory of whatever is happening at that time. Plus, being a writer, it goes with the territory.

Ferrari World: There is money and then there is wealth! Ladies and Gentlemen, Denise Mose has seen and felt WEALTH. I heard about Ferrari World because this is where all of the very famous get their customed vehicles done. Can you imagine? Just ordering a Ferrari and being able to pay not for one, but a few? Knowing this, Aadil and I were off to see all the wonders it held. Although it is mostly an indoor amusement park, its rather awesome to behold. It is the first Ferrari-branded theme park and has the record for largest space frame structure ever built. When you get on this roller coaster, the actual car is a Ferrari. Isn't that insane? Just go, you'll love it.

Emirates Palace: You see it before you get there. However, that is the nature for all things Dubai. The foreshadowing is simply jaw-dropping. Gold...Gold...and more Gold! We parked the car and walked towards the palace. The image that still sticks in my head is the many trashcans that were outside. These were no ordinary litter bins, people. No, they were much more. I never knew that 24-carat trash cans existed until i went to the palace. After all, it cost about three billion dollars to build so why wouldn't they have gold trash cans? Also, the beautiful water streaming down outside just speaks of luxury. As if that wasn't enough, something else caught my eye: Upon getting a closer look, my mouth dropped again. I noticed the automated teller machine (ATM) - Except, it was rather...Big! Well, that's because it was a Gold Bar Machine. Dubai is so wealthy, they dispense gold bars for those who can afford them. WHAT???

Since, I arrived around Christmas, the trees were decorated and fake snow was everywhere. Dubai is a tropical country and it was a warm 90 degrees outside. The staff were pretty people. Their outfits were uniform, yet extremely stylish. I simply walked through the palace and made sure to close my mouth because around every corner was something else to be marveled. I let my phone take as many pictures as it could handle...

Atlantis The Palm: The next day, I knew I would be seeing this extravagant hotel. First, the aerial view is iconic. Therefore, I knew I was going to investigate a helicopter tour. This luxury hotel has everything...And I do mean everything. It is based off the myth, Atlantis; however, there are purposeful Arabian elements. There are many things to see at Atlantis, but you must see the aquarium. Geez, where do I begin? Dolphins, sharks, assorted fish and the most incredible landscape to see. It's utter fantasy! Plus, if you have enough money, you can get an aquarium room as your suite. From the lobby to the ceiling, it is a masterpiece to behold.

Helicopter Tour: Since this was my last trip, I was going out with a bang! I set my sites on a chopper. Nothing says "Big Balling" like a helicopter over Dubai! Hey, you only live once, right? I went to the front desk and booked my excursion. Although it was only 12 minutes, it was not cheap. But hey, broke people don't visit Dubai, do they? I absolutely loved the convenience of the tour picking me up and dropping me off. I decided to eat a light breakfast because I didn't want to "see" my food so soon. We arrived at the Dubai Police Academy and were immediately weighed. The helicopter was small, so whoever you flew with had to match the weight of the flight. I am rather small and was told that my seat would be up front. Yippee! Who wants to see Dubai from the back row? My turn soon came, and I liked my pilot the moment he smiled at me. He gave us some safety precautions, headsets and then we were in the air. It was better than I could have ever imagined. On the tour we saw the Palm Jumeirah, Burj Arab, Burj Khalifa, Jumeirah Beach, Dubai Canal, beautiful homes and shopping malls. Tim, the pilot, had so much information and we asked him just as many questions. Being the good American that I am, I recorded everything and posted it to social media the moment we touched ground. What a day, but it wasn't over yet...

Yacht Ride: Ahhhhh! I got back from the helicopter and went straight to my room. I took a nap, showered, had lunch and waited for my final tour. This was my last day in Dubai and there was no better way to end it then by being on the water at sunset. Why stop at a helicopter? Of course, my tour picked me up and took me to the beautiful docks. I showed my ticket and they escorted me to my yacht. Whoa, she was gorgeous! Two men served as the captain and co-captain. The chef introduced himself and gave me two menus for food. I was about to be in tears, because I knew it would be hard to say good-bye to Dubai. What a perfect day to be on the water. The ride was so calming and they left me alone to take in the astounding views.

I sat towards the front of the yacht and perched myself on the seated railing. Looking out, seeing blue water and feeling the mist was magical. I was here in Dubai. Me, a Southern chick from Alabama. Society might say, "What was I doing traveling there?" The South has its own stereotypes and that is one of the many reasons why I wanted to take this year abroad in the first place. Denise Yvette Mose is a strong person. I didn't know how strong that lady was until she moved on the other side of the world. You know what? I'm so very proud of her. After three glasses of champagne, food, epic pictures and life reflections, we journeyed back to the dock. Aadil was there to take me to my hotel. As I sat in my room preparing to pack, tears silently fell down my face. My seven days in Dubai were complete.

It's Almost Over...Packing Up

December...In less than 30 days, I would be back in the United States. Tina did her best to keep me another year. I turned her down. I came and did what I set out to do. Nouchelle was proud and I was all the richer for coming to China. My flight was booked and my last few classes were scheduled. Christy was hired as my replacement and I trained her to do my job. Although she was nervous, I told her not to worry.

Here's the thing: Y'all, it flew by! Like, I remember packing for China and here I was packing to LEAVE China. It was crazy. All of my memories of this insane leap were nearly done, and a sense of melancholy washed over me. A time or two, I thought about extending my stay in China because leaving suddenly became very overwhelming. This was my normal now: Wake up, study my Mandarin, order my rice bread, office work, prepare my class, lunch, teach, go home. It was simple and I loved it. Was I really going to say good-bye? People extended all the time. Tina wanted me to stay, so why not? Right?

Yet, a few things were pulling at my heart...Family. My beautiful family. I missed seeing my dad's face. If you ever met my dad, you'd say he had a charming face. Danielle is my identical twin and thanks to social media, I got to see her nearly every day. Madison is my niece and such a funny little lady. She is all arms and legs, perfect for her budding tennis career. My big brother Danny...What do I say about him? He has the best advice and has never once judged any of my decisions. My best friend John Lennard made sure to keep me laughing, especially on days when homesickness hit me hard.

I took China for what it was...Life-Changing! I would hold onto this experience and apply it for whatever was headed my way. You don't spend a year away living on another continent and remain the same. I was eager to see what Denise Yvette Mose would do next.

Korea

My trip home was going great. I was on my flight and enjoying the movie I had just selected. Three hours into my flight, the pilot comes on the speaker and mentions that we must land. We would all be spending the night due to a plane malfunction. Ok, I dealt with this on my way over to China. Therefore, I was ready for anything. Turns out, we were staying in Korea! Whoa! I got to check another place off my bucket list.

We landed in Korea and I collected all my luggage. The nearest hotel was actually in the airport and that's where I decided to bunk for the night. The airline had offered us another place to stay so if we chose a different location, the fee was on us. No big deal, I was going for convenience.

Since it was only 6pm in the evening, I decided to find the nearest hotel by my gate. We were scheduled to fly to the USA in the morning. As fate would have it, Incheon Airport Transit Hotel was right around the corner. By this point, I had changed a lot of my money back into US Currency. However, I kept quite a bit of Renminbi (RMB) as souvenirs and pieces to show my family.

I approached the front desk and they had a myriad of ways to pay for your room. I asked for the Korean rate as opposed to the US rate. No question, I paid my room in my native dollar. The hotel boasted a wonderful buffet that overlooked the rest of the airport.

I loved my room. Here we go, another pinch-me moment. Who doesn't want to visit Seoul, Korea? The airport itself was quite beautiful. There was a lot of Western culture influences, so I felt right at home. Although I knew my time here would be brief, I decided to go ahead and buy a t-shirt with the matching keychain.

The food was calling me, and I could no longer deny my tummy. A bevy of deliciousness was at my beck and call and I answered! Desserts and coffee were on the other side, so I quickly found my way there. After two good helpings, I went back to my room. The time was getting late and I did not want to miss my flight. After a nice long shower, I watched a bit of television, took several more pictures and went to sleep.

In the morning, I arrived at my gate and grabbed coffee. As I sat in the airport, it hit me that these were my last moments of living in the Far East. Once I boarded that plane for America, it was over.

A single tear ran down my face...

Touchdown

"Please gather all of your belongings and welcome to Huntsville."

The flight attendant said those final words. Was I really home? Looking out at the familiar surroundings let me know that I was indeed back in my hometown. I was happy, but I wasn't...

How do I go back to normal? Was THIS my normal now?

Danielle and Maddie picked me up and they looked the same, but they didn't...

For a second, I thought I was losing it a bit. After all, I hadn't actually seen these faces for over a year. Honestly, I was having a sort of out-of-body experience. Where were my students? Where was Ivy, my roommate? Why didn't I have my morning rice bread for breakfast? No one spoke Chinese!

I was home.

My twin caught on and quickly told me to get in the truck. I laugh about this now because she knew exactly what was happening to me. Twenty years ago, she moved to Europe and lived in Paris, France, for four years. When she returned to the USA, she was a bit lost, too.

My family had prepared a huge feast for me when I went to see them. Everyone came to see me and they had so many questions. Of course, I was happy to share about every experience. That was a fun night.

I had really traveled by Blind Faith...

Afterword

Being a big brother offers one a real perspective of people. By people, I mean siblings. My parents had three children: Yours Truly was first, Danielle followed and six minutes later, Denise chose to arrive. The home our parents made for us was full of love, laughter and lessons that we will cherish. Denise's first book was titled, *Life at 433*, referencing the residence of our childhood home. Here we are, several books later and Denise asked (more like told) me to write a brief synopsis of her experience abroad in Asia.

Like anyone, I had my reservations. She didn't know anyone there, nor did she speak the language. So, why go? If you know my sister Denise, it's more like, "I HAVE TO GO!" Life is short people, who wants to regret something that could turn out to be rather awesome. Well, you know how that story ended. She loved her time there and saw many other countries and historical sites as well.

I have no idea where her path will lead her. All I know is that she will take it on like everything she does. Congrats, Nese. I'm proud of you and love you very much.

Big Brother,

Daniel Mose, III

www.ingramcontent.com/pod-product-compliance
Lightning Source LLC
Chambersburg PA
CBHW071410290426
44108CB00014B/1768